LEARN PATCHWORK

Lynette~Merlin Syme

THE MAIN STREET PRESS • PITTSTOWN, NEW JERSEY

The author and publishers acknowledge the help and co-operation of the following companies, designers, organisations and individuals:
Sir Tatton Sykes, Sledmere, for the use of Sledmere's gardens and grounds
The Church of England Children's Society and Laura Ashley plc, for permission to reproduce photographs of patchworks on pages 11, 21, 35, 38, 45, 58, 60 from the 1984-85 patchwork competition
Members of the London Quilters, for permission to photograph their designs:
Jane Plowman (Hexagon quilt, page 14; Friendship quilt, page 56)
Norah Field (Miniature patchwork, page 17)
Eve May (Log Cabin quilt, page 25; Puffed patchwork eiderdown, page 53; Crazy quilt, page 55)
Pamela Cross (Patchwork jacket, page 30; Red carry bag, page 42)
Jill Meeson (Clamshell needlework tidy, page 49)
The Jane Austen Memorial Trust, Chawton, Hampshire, for permission to reproduce the photograph of Jane Austen's quilt by J. Butler-Kearney, on page 37
Jennifer Hollingdale, for permission to photograph her designs on pages 18 and 26
Jem Patchwork Templates (distributed by Atlascraft), for supplying templates
Dried flowers by Jane Thompson, Bromley, Kent
Child's lace dress by Pat Smith, Hungerford, Berkshire

First American Edition 1987

Published by
The Main Street Press, Inc.
William Case House
Pittstown, New Jersey 08867

Published originally by
William Collins Sons & Co Ltd
London, England

Designed and edited by TL Creative Services
Series Editor Eve Harlow
Photography by Di Lewis
Illustrations by Terry Evans

Printed by New Interlitho, Italy

Contents

Introduction

Patchwork has been a popular needlecraft for many years, although it has its origins in poverty and hardship and the need to make do and mend. The craft helped to stimulate courage in the early American settler women, sharpening their observation of surroundings and developing their creativity. In Britain, where the roots of American patchwork are found, the craft took a different direction, becoming more formal and exact in design and execution. Today, patchwork is still a needlecraft for everyone, no matter what their lifestyle − or age − and its appeal continues undiminished.

Learn Patchwork is a book for beginners but experienced needlewomen will also find a wealth of ideas and inspiration in these pages. Some of the designs were made available by the Church of England Children's Society and Laura Ashley plc, which together ran a patchwork competition with the aim of furthering and maintaining interest in this traditional craft. Other designs are by members of the London Quilters. The designers and organisations have the grateful thanks and appreciation of the author and the publishers.

All about Patchwork

Patchwork has its beginnings in the need to make do and mend, but the fascination of modern patchwork lies in creating individual patterns and colour schemes using only the simplest sewing techniques. This chapter explains the basic equipment necessary and the first steps in patchwork.

The history

It is almost certain that patchwork, which is acknowledged to have been in existence for over 3,000 years, started off in the poorer homes, where there was a very real need to make do and mend, and where no piece of fabric, however small, was thrown away. Only as late as the eighteenth century did patchwork join the crafts and skills of embroidery to become a leisure occupation for the ladies of the middle classes.

While patchwork is widely considered to be American in origin — indeed, it is almost possible to write a history of North America by making a study of its quilts — this is by no means so. The early English pioneers made extensive use of patchwork techniques from necessity because ships from home brought tools and seed, with little cargo space for non-essentials, such as fabrics and threads. The American people went on to develop their own special forms of patchwork, which today are referred to as 'piecing' or 'piecework'.

During the 1920s an archeological dig in the region of the River Ganges unearthed several pieces of patchwork which were estimated to date between the sixth and ninth century AD. They revealed some interesting facts, the most important being that in those days patchwork was made in exactly the same way as it is now, using the same stitch. One of the patchworks unearthed was made in silks, theoretically by a priest with pieces left for his use by travellers or pilgrims. The work is remarkable not only in colour and

design, but that it has survived in spite of being made of silk, a fabric that has notoriously poor lasting properties.

When, in the eighteenth century, patchwork became a recreation, velvets and silks were often mixed together. The velvets, being considerably heavier, pulled on the silks and destroyed them, so comparatively little work survives from this period.

Making patchwork

Patchwork is an ideal way of making use of all those little pieces of fabric that have been hoarded away because they were far too pretty to throw out. You will probably find that you can make a whole bedspread without buying a single piece of fabric (except for the lining), and dressmaker friends will, undoubtedly, be pleased to help you with supplies of fabric. Alternatively, you can encourage them to join you and pool your resources. There is a lot to be said for this method of working when it is possible to share ideas, experiences and mistakes, as well as to gain inspiration from other people's work.

Once you have mastered the

This double-size quilt was a group project and has been made with twenty 30cm (12in) blocks set around a central panel and borders. The blocks are based on a traditional American pattern — the Saw-toothed Star or Simple Star — which is a nine-patch block design. The central star is worked in appliqué. Triangles, squares and rhomboids make up the various areas of the quilt, and quilting has been worked to add interest and texture to the design

Patchwork templates

Here is the range of patchwork templates available in shops in pairs, a metal for cutting papers and a plastic window template for cutting fabrics. The arrows on the shapes illustrated indicate the direction of the straight grain of fabric when fabric patches are being cut.

Hexagon A six-sided shape with 120° angles. It can be used alone or with other shapes that have 120° or 60° angles.

Rectangle Half or one-third of a square, with 90° angles.

Square Can be divided into rectangles or triangles.

Diamond Also known as the Lozenge Diamond, with two 60° and two 120° angles.

Long Diamond A longer diamond shape than the lozenge, with two 45° and two 135° angles.

Triangle Three sides of equal length and 60° angles.

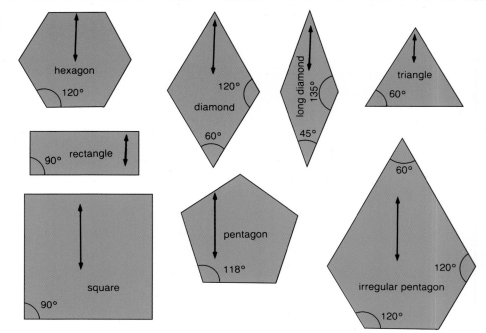

technique of applying fabric to paper you will find that the work progresses very fast. However, it is worth taking time initially to learn the correct technique, so that corners are firm and accurate. Nothing shouts quite so loudly as corners that do not quite meet, and no amount of beautiful stitching will cover up this fault.

It is a common fallacy to think that a first piece should be made with a large patch. For instance, a 10cm (4in) square will be more difficult to handle than a 2.5cm (1in) hexagon.

Skill in needlework is not one of the requirements for making patchwork, since one stitch only is used: a simple, small, oversewing stitch, which can quickly be mastered.

An eye for colour is a bonus in your favour. Many of you will have had some experience of achieving the right balance of colour in a room, and you will not necessarily have had a totally free hand – you may have had to work within certain colour limitations. So with patchwork: you may have a lot of fabrics but they may be of predominantly one colour. By purchasing a piece of fabric in a different or toning colour you will probably find that you can transform the rather ordinary item you intended to make into something very special.

Materials and equipment

You will probably find that you have all the tools you need in your sewing box, with a few exceptions.

Templates

Templates are the accurate patterns from which the fabric and paper are cut. (The fabric is mounted on the paper while it is worked into the design.) Most good craft shops sell various shapes of template, but if they are not available it is relatively easy to make your own out of good quality card, using a steel ruler, protractor, pair of compasses and a sharp crafts knife (see page 64).

Templates are sold in packs of two. One is solid metal, which is used as a template for cutting out papers and is the size of the finished patch (Fig 1a). The second template is larger by 6mm (¼in) all round, to allow for seams (Fig 1b). The central part is clear plastic, so that when the template is placed over the piece of fabric the portion of a pattern that will appear on the finished patch can be clearly seen. By moving the template over the fabric you can find the area you want on your patch and centralise it (Fig 2).

In patchwork, when referring to a certain size patch, for instance, a

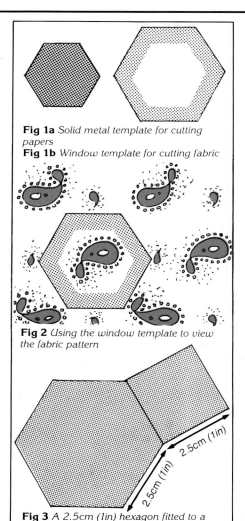

Fig 1a *Solid metal template for cutting papers*
Fig 1b *Window template for cutting fabric*

Fig 2 *Using the window template to view the fabric pattern*

Fig 3 *A 2.5cm (1in) hexagon fitted to a 2.5cm (1in) square*

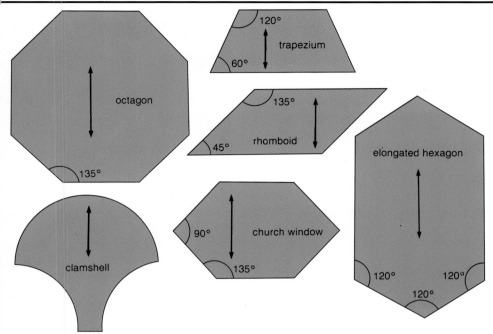

Pentagon A five-sided shape with 118° angles. It cannot be used alone to make patchwork.
Irregular Pentagon A diamond with a section 'trimmed' away, forming a shape with one 60° and four 120° angles.
Octagon An eight-sided shape with 135° angles. It must be worked with a square of the same size.
Clamshell This shape is always used alone but patterns can be built up with it.
Trapezium A half hexagon shape with two 120° and two 60° angles.
Rhomboid A shape formed with two irregular triangles, long edges making the sides of the rhomboid. The finer angle is 45° and the wider 135°.
Church Window Also called the Long Hexagon, with six equal sides, four angles of 135° and two of 90°.
Elongated Hexagon Also called the Coffin, with two sides of the same length and four sides of a different length. The angles are 120°.

2.5cm (1in) hexagon, this means that one side of the metal hexagon template has that measurement. Thus it is possible to mix a 2.5cm (1in) hexagon with a 2.5cm (1in) square (Fig 3).

Scissors
You will need two pairs of scissors: one for cutting out the paper shapes (paper blunts scissors very quickly so keep them just for that purpose) and a sharp pair for cutting out the fabric. You may find a pair of small embroidery scissors is also useful, for snipping thread when sewing patches together.

Thread
The traditionalists would observe the rule of using black or white cotton thread for all fabrics except silk, and silk thread in those two colours for dealing with all silks. Unless your stitching is near perfect it is preferable to use a selection of colours. Cotton thread, Nos. 50 or 60, is ideal unless you are working with silk fabric, when you should use silk thread. Synthetic thread is not advisable as you cannot work it into small, tight stitches.

Needles
As you will be working very small, neat stitches, your needles should be fine: Nos. 9 or 10 'sharps' are best,

although many prefer to use what are known as 'betweens'. These needles are usually favoured by tailors and are readily available. They are much shorter and so do not bend as easily. However, with experience you will find out for yourself what suits you. You may find that the best method is to start with a large needle and progress to a shorter, finer needle as you become more confident.

Thimble
Do try to become used to wearing a thimble. Without one you will find that, working with paper in your fabric, your middle finger will become punctured and very sore!

Pins
Sharp, thin pins are essential. Buy glass-headed pins (made by manufacturers from discarded needles), which are excellent and easily seen when dropped.

Paper
Good quality writing paper is used for making templates. Do not use shiny paper as the template will slip while you are working the patch. You should be able to feel the edge of the paper through the fabric when you are working the patch. Postcards are also suitable, but make sure that they are all of the same weight otherwise the size of your patches will vary.

Other tools
As well as these basic tools, you may find it useful to have an unpicking tool, double-sided adhesive tape, beeswax for strengthening thread, a pair of compasses, a crafts knife and a steel ruler (which is easier to use with a crafts knife or wheel than a plastic one). Squared paper and isometric paper (ruled vertically and diagonally) are ideal for making designs, together with pencils and felt-tipped pens.

Fabrics
Be selective with fabrics. Begin by sorting your hoard into fabrics of a similar weight and texture. Discard nylon fabrics and fabrics that will fray badly or are so thin that your turnings will be seen through the finished work. Discard, too, those fabrics with a high synthetic content: these are difficult to crease and to make into neat patches with good, flat corners and straight edges. Tightly woven dress cottons are ideal; so, too, are the semi-glazed cottons used for furnishings.

Mixing fabric textures and weights must come with practice. A patch made of cotton fabric will make a different finished size from one made of velvet. It is possible to compensate for the difference in weight by mounting the thinner fabric on to a bonding fabric and working the two as one, but this is more advanced work and should not be tried on a first piece.

Next, consider the item you would like to make. Bear in mind that if you are going to all the trouble of making, say, a quilt, you will want it to last for some time. If, on the other hand, you are making a fashion garment, you can disregard the fact that silky fabrics will not wear so well when used with tweeds and wools. Longevity will not be one of your considerations, rather colour, texture and overall eye-appeal.

Basic techniques
Making paper shapes
The basic geometric shapes used in patchwork – square, rectangle, hexagon, octagon and diamond – are, in essence, treated in the same way. The hexagon is used to demonstrate the basic techniques.

Cut out the papers, using the solid metal template, making sure the sides are straight and the corners accurate.

There are three ways of cutting the papers. You can hold the paper in

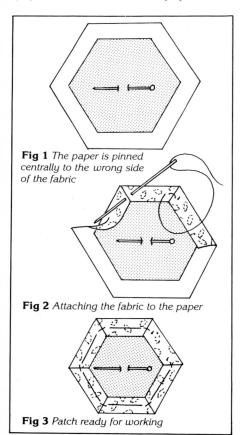

Fig 1 *The paper is pinned centrally to the wrong side of the fabric*

Fig 2 *Attaching the fabric to the paper*

Fig 3 *Patch ready for working*

your hand, with the solid template held firmly over it, and cut round the shape with scissors, keeping the blades as straight as possible against the edges. You can cut several thicknesses at once but do not try to cut out too many in this way. It is difficult to maintain the correct angle with the scissors and you may find that the bottom papers are a different size from the top ones.

The second method is to draw round the template with a sharp pencil and then cut round the pencilled outline. If you are using this method take care to keep the pencil sharp and placed tight to the template.

The third method involves using a crafts knife. You will need a board on to which you can cut. Place your crafts knife next to the template on the paper and cut round. Alternatively, pencil the outline first, then cut out the shape with the knife, pressing against a steel ruler.

Whichever method you use, and all are equally successful, make sure the same method is used throughout the piece you are working, to avoid any variation in the finished size of the patches. It is a good idea to experiment with all the methods to find out which one suits you best.

Mounting patches
Now choose the colours and patterns you want to work with from your collection of fabrics, and cut out several pieces, using the clear window template. Make sure that at least one side of the template is placed on the straight grain of fabric.

Take the first piece of fabric and pin a paper centrally to it, on the wrong side (Fig 1). With this in one hand and a threaded needle in the other, fold one side of fabric down over the paper so that you can feel a firm edge made by the paper through the fabric. Run your thumb and index finger across the edge to make a sharp fold. Turn the paper in your hand so that you can work the next side (Fig 2).

Having made your fold in the same way, insert your needle under the fabric just short of the pleat made at the junction of these two sides. Slide your needle under the fabric – but not through the paper – and bring it

Flower pincushions
The pretty pincushions, looking like colourful flowers, would make an ideal first patchwork project. Each pincushion has only 14 patches so it is completed quite quickly and any scraps of fabric can be used. When finished, you will have a useful sewing accessory for your needlework basket.

Make two rosettes of hexagons using a 2.5cm *(1in)* template (see page

out on the other side of the fold. Do this fairly close to the cut edge of the fabric: if you stitch too close to the point of the corner, the stitch will not have enough retaining power and the paper will fall out. Take your needle back to where you first inserted it and make a second stitch over the first. The corner is now anchored.

Fold the fabric on the third side

making it easier to line up one corner with another when working them. It is, in fact, a great help to have an iron to hand at all times when working.

When working patchwork it is advisable to leave the papers in the fabric patches for as long as possible (quite a few will fall out with the handling of the piece of work), as they help to keep the shape and, particularly with a large piece, avoid unnecessary creasing. Do not reuse the papers: they will not have enough body second time around to give you an accurate shape.

Cutting thread

Always cut your thread – breaking it also weakens it. Cotton thread is made up of tiny filaments spun together and there is a nap to it. For this reason, thread your needle with the end that comes off the reel first, and make a knot where you cut. Do not be tempted to thread your needle with too long a length of thread. The constant friction as it is worked through the material will also weaken it, causing it to snap. If you run the thread over a piece of beeswax, knots and tangles will be avoided and the thread strengthened.

Planning colour schemes

When you have made several patches, lay them out on a flat surface and move them around until you are happy with the balance of colour and the mixture of plain and patterned fabrics. In this way, you will also be able to see whether you could add another colour to advantage or perhaps remove something. If you are working on a large project you may wish to pin each piece in place to a backing fabric – for instance, an old sheet – so that you can maintain your design in place over a period of time, removing each piece as it is required for sewing. For smaller projects you may find it helpful to pin patches to a soft board, such as a cork bathmat.

12 for technique) and finish them as instructed on page 10. Pin the rosettes together, wrong sides facing. Oversew all round the 'petals', leaving the seam between two 'petals' open. Stuff firmly with polyester filling to make a rounded pincushion. Close the open seam with oversewing.

The round pincushion in the picture is an example of miniature patchwork and is made with 12mm (½in) hexagons. Both sides of the

pincushion are the same, made up with 13 hexagons in pale blue fabric (with 12 half hexagons set into the edges to form a circular shape) and six hexagons in a floral fabric. The pincushion has a 15mm (⅝in) gusset and is piped with the same pale blue fabric.

This hexagon design could also be worked as a full-size cushion. For a 25cm (10in) diameter cushion use 31mm (1¼in) hexagons.

and work the corner in the same way as the first. Continue round the template until all corners are secured. It is not necessary to cut the thread between corners (Fig 3).

Remove the retaining pin and you should find that the paper is firmly lodged inside the fabric, even though you have not sewn through the paper. The advantage of this method

is that at the end of the work it is simple to remove the papers with thumb and forefinger.

Finishing patches

You will find it an advantage to press the patches before you start sewing them together. In this way, the corners will lie flat and the angles formed by the corners will be sharp,

Joining patches

You are now ready to start joining patches together. To do this small oversewing stitches are used, ideally about 16–20 stitches per 2.5cm (1in), picking up just a few threads of the

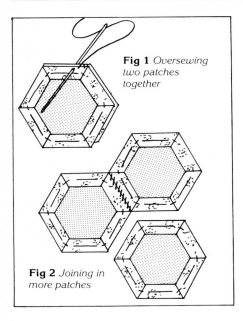

Fig 1 *Oversewing two patches together*

Fig 2 *Joining in more patches*

material but allowing the needle to glance over the edge of the paper.

Place two patches together, right sides facing (Fig 1). Start sewing about 1.5mm (¹⁄₁₆ in) in from one corner and work back towards the corner, sewing over the points twice to make sure they are firmly together. Now work across the complete side of these two patches till you reach the next corner. Oversew the corner twice and then work back 1.5mm (¹⁄₁₆ in). Make a double stitch and cut off the thread.

You are now ready to join in the next patch. Open and flatten the two joined patches and decide where the next patch is to be joined. Place the new patch on the chosen patch, right sides facing and aligning edges, and start sewing 1.5mm (¹⁄₁₆ in) from the corner as before. Continue in the same way, joining in patches (Fig 2).

Finishing patchwork

Do not remove papers until all the patches have been joined. There is no need to remove the basting stitches. The stitches hold the raw edges of fabric down through wear and subsequent laundering.

You now have a piece of patchworked fabric and this is used to make items in exactly the same way as any other piece of fabric. If special techniques, such as lining or interlining the patchwork, are required, these are indicated in the project instructions.

Basket of sachets

Lozenge diamond patches joined together into star shapes make pretty sachets. Filled with lavender and finished with a ribbon loop, they can be hung in cupboards to perfume clothes or linens. Line a basket with patchwork and fill it with sachets for a charming bedroom accessory.

Basket

The basket measures 26×20cm (10¼ × 8in) and 43 hexagons worked with a 21mm (⅞in) template have been joined together to make the lining (Fig 1). There are 17 patches in plain pink fabric, 18 in white sprigged fabric and eight in pink sprigged fabric.

Catch the edges of the finished patchwork to the inner rim of the basket and finish the edge with a strip of embroidered rosebud trim.

Sachets

Each sachet requires 18 lozenge diamonds worked with a 2.5cm (1in) template, six joined to make a star shape for the front, six for the back and six inserted into the angle between the star's points, joining front to back (Figs 2, 3, 4).

Leave one seam open, turn the sachet to the right side and pour in sweet, dried herbs or lavender through a paper funnel. Close the open seam with slipstitches.

Trim with a 30cm (12in) length of narrow satin ribbon folded as shown in the picture, and sew a single embroidered rosebud over the crossed ribbon ends.

If fine fabrics are used, the filling may show through. In this case, cut the fabric diamonds and then use the same template to cut diamonds from thin white fabric. Baste the two shapes together and mount on papers as one.

Fig 1 *43 hexagons worked with a 21mm (⅞in) template, sewn together to make a lining for a 26×20cm (10¼ × 8in) basket*

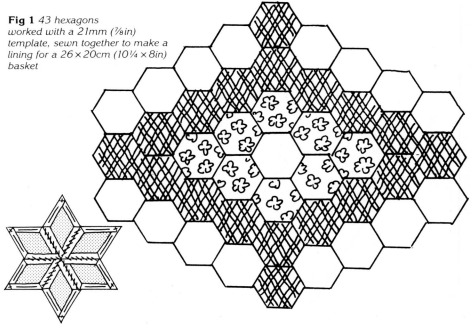

Fig 2 *Six lozenge diamonds worked with a 2.5cm (1in) template, sewn together to make a star shape, from the wrong side of work*

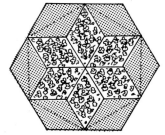

Fig 3 *Diamonds are sewn into the angles between the star's points to join front to back. Fold the side patches on the dotted line*

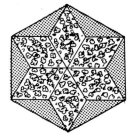

Fig 4 *The finished sachet*

Hexagons

The hexagon has six equal sides with 120° angles and can be used to form a number of patterns and designs without the need to introduce another patchwork shape. Hexagons are most associated with English patchwork and are the easiest shape to work with.

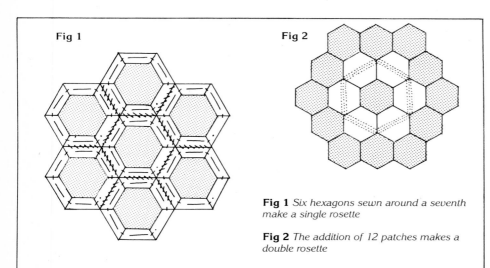

Fig 1

Fig 2

Fig 1 Six hexagons sewn around a seventh make a single rosette

Fig 2 The addition of 12 patches makes a double rosette

Table mats

The table mats in the picture are made with 2.5cm *(1in)* hexagons. The techniques for mounting hexagon patches and joining them together are shown on pages 8-10.

Sew six hexagons around a seventh to make a rosette (Fig 1), then add another 12 hexagons to make a double rosette (Fig 2).

Finish the patchwork (see page 10), then, using it as a pattern, cut the same shape from plain lining fabric, adding 6mm *(¼ in)* seam allowance all round. Turn in the seam allowance and oversew the lining to the wrong side of the patchwork.

Designs with hexagons

Hexagons are a favourite shape for making quilts, sometimes used in a pattern formation and sometimes at random. One of the most popular patterns is Grandmother's Flower Garden (Fig 1).

In this, rosettes are made with hexagons of flowered fabrics surrounding a central patch in a plain colour. The double rosette hexagons are traditionally cut from green fabric to represent foliage. These double rosettes are then joined by white fabric hexagons to represent the paths between the flower beds.

This pretty pattern is sometimes adapted to other forms; the quilt on page 14, for instance, is made up of double rosettes adapted to elongated rosettes.

The Garland (Fig 2) makes an ideal border for a quilt, or it could be used to edge a skirt. If it is being used to edge a quilt worked with double rosettes, the Garland's rosettes could be increased to doubles.

Ocean Wave (Fig 3) is another possible edging pattern and is traditionally worked in toning colours, the palest on the inner row and the darkest on the outer.

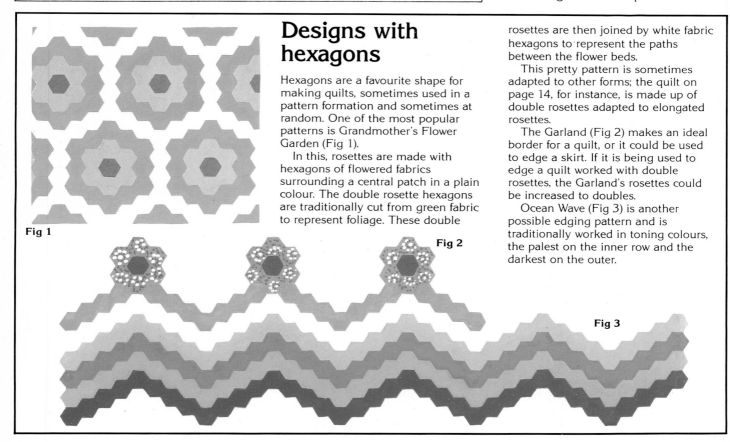

Fig 1

Fig 2

Fig 3

Flower garden quilt

This modern hexagon-patch quilt is made with elongated rosettes (Fig 1), a variation on the way hexagons are usually used for quilts. Each rosette is made up of 25 hexagons and, like the traditional Grandmother's Flower Garden design, white patches are used to represent the paths between the flower beds.

Fig 1 *Elongated rosette made up of 25 hexagons*

Patches required

Finished size 279×241cm (110×95in) including border
Using a 2.5cm *(1in)* hexagon template: 2000 coloured patches; 880 white patches

Working the design

Make up 68 elongated rosettes, each with a plain-coloured patch in the middle. Join white hexagons between rosettes when making up the quilt. Work half rosettes for the edges of the quilt and quarter rosettes for the corners (Fig 2).

Finishing

The quilt in the picture is mounted on white fabric, turned on to the edges of the patchwork, making 10cm *(4in)* borders. The quilt has lines of quilting stitches along the 'paths' and through the patches of the rosettes (see page 16 for techniques).

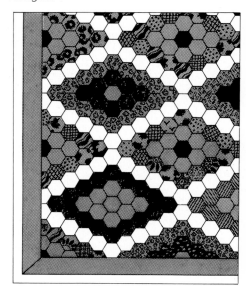

Fig 2 *A corner of the quilt, showing half elongated rosettes at the edges and a quarter rosette at the corner*

Right: Hand-sewn quilting has been worked through the centre line of the hexagons in a diamond pattern to secure the patchwork to its backing and give the quilt better handle

Estimating fabric quantities

Working out how much fabric is required for patchworks using diamonds or hexagons need not cause problems if you follow this method of calculating.

Having chosen the template — say it is a hexagon — first measure across the widest part of the window template (the one with which you cut fabric). A 2.5cm *(1in)* hexagon measures 6.5cm *(2½in)* between its widest points (Fig 1). From 91cm *(36in)*-wide fabric, therefore, 14 hexagons can be obtained from the width.

Now measure the template between the parallel sides — on the 2.5cm *(1in)* hexagon this measurement will be

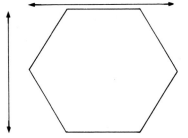

Fig 1 *Measure the hexagon between its widest points, then between the parallel sides*

6cm *(2¼in)*. From a 91cm *(36in)* length of fabric, 15 hexagons can be cut from the depth. Thus, from a piece of fabric 91cm *(36in)* square, 210 2.5cm *(1in)* hexagons can be obtained.

Finishing quilts

After the patchwork has been completed, quilts should be lined and the edges finished.

Lining

For a double bed quilt it may be necessary to join pieces of lining fabric to achieve the desired width. It is preferable to join widths so that there is no seam down the middle of the quilt. Divide one width and seam the half-widths to the sides of the main piece. When lining very wide quilts, join as many pieces as required but always try to have a single width in the middle.

Interlining

You may want to have an interlining between the patchwork and the lining, particularly if you are planning to quilt the patchwork. Interlining can simply be a pre-shrunk blanket, or use cotton or polyester wadding, which is available for this purpose.

Attaching the lining

Spread the patchwork on the floor, wrong side up. Mark the middle of each of the four sides with pins. Mark the lining in the same way, then spread the lining on top of the patchwork, right side up. Pin the two layers together, first down the centre, smoothing the lining towards the edges as you pin. Then pin across from side to side, again smoothing the lining to the edges. If the quilt is very large you may need to pin in thirds or even quarters.

The easiest way to stitch the lining to the patchwork is to turn the edges of the patchwork to the wrong side and baste. Turn under the edges of the lining so that it falls short of the patchwork by a scant 3mm (1/8in). Hem the lining to the patchwork.

If a narrow edge of the lining is to show (such as on the Crazy Patchwork quilt on page 54), cut the lining 2.5–3cm (1–1 1/4in) larger all round and turn a hem on to the patchwork. Machine-stitch or hand-hem the edges.

Before the pins are removed the lining should be tied to the patchwork (see Working Quilt Ties).

Borders

To work a fabric border, decide on the finished width and double this measurement, adding 2.5cm (1in). Measure the length and width of the quilt.

Cut and join strips so that you have sufficient for two long sides and two short sides plus 5cm (2in) on each length. Fold and press each strip lengthwise. Apply a strip along one side of the quilt, right sides facing and matching edges. Machine-stitch about 12mm (1/2in) from the edge (Fig 1). Fold the strip on its crease to the wrong side and hem to the lining. Apply the second strip, with the extra 2.5cm (1in) extending over the edge of the quilt. Machine-stitch as before (Fig 2). Fold the strip to the wrong side and hem, then tuck in the end of the strip, press and slipstitch neatly (Fig 3).

Working quilt ties

Tying the lining to the patchwork is a time-consuming process but it is essential to prevent the ballooning that would otherwise occur.

The pins holding the patchwork to the lining should still be in position. Strengthen a long length of No.24 cotton thread by pulling it over beeswax. Thread a needle and, working from the lining side, take a 6mm (1/4in) stitch through both thicknesses of fabric, leaving a 10cm (4in) end. Take another stitch in the same place and cut the thread with a 10cm (4in) end. Tie the two ends together securely. Cut off the excess thread, not too close to the knot. Work ties at 23cm (9in) intervals across and along the quilt.

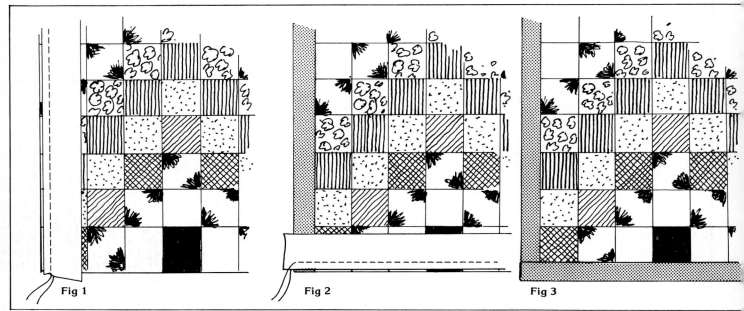

Fig 1 *Apply the first strip to one side of the quilt, stitching about 12mm (1/2in) from the edge*

Fig 2 *Fold the strip to the wrong side and hem. Then apply the second strip, overlapping the end and extending about 2.5cm (1in)*

Fig 3 *Fold the second strip to the wrong side and hem, then tuck in the open end and neaten with slipstitches*

A very pretty effect can be achieved by using 1.5mm (1/16in)-wide satin ribbon for ties, finishing the double knot on the right side of the quilt.

Quilting

A decorative effect (and better handle) is achieved by quilting. Traditionally, quilting is worked with running stitches but some patchworkers prefer to use a sewing-machine for speed.

To prepare the quilt, pin quilt, interlining and lining together, with the interlining sandwiched between wrong sides of quilt and lining. Baste the quilt from top to bottom, side to side and from corner to corner diagonally, through all thicknesses. Remove the pins.

Quilting designs can be impressed on the lining side of the quilt using a blunt-tipped needle, drawing the needle along a ruler or along the lines of a design drawn on tracing paper. Alternatively, use a 'pouncing' technique as follows. Pierce the lines of the tracing design with a pin, making holes about 3mm (1/8in) apart. Pin the tracing to the lining side of the quilt. Powder a little chalk or charcoal. Rub the powder along the holes so that a little goes through on to the fabric. Remove the tracing and draw over the line with a chalk pencil.

To work quilting properly, a quilting frame should be used because the stitch is made with a stabbing technique, passing the needle through with one hand and passing it back up through the quilt with the other. However, many quilters work without a frame and use a continuous running stitch.

Using No.50 cotton thread in a colour matching the patchwork as closely as possible, work neat, even-sized running stitches along the lines of the design, through all thicknesses of fabric. Thread ends should not be knotted. Begin and end with a double backstitch, leaving an end of thread. Re-thread the needle and draw the ends into the work.

The edging of the quilt is applied after quilting has been completed. There is no need to tie the quilt as quilting does the job of holding the patchwork to the lining.

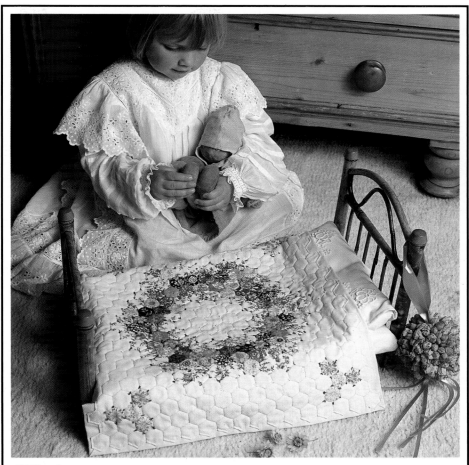

Miniature patchwork

If you like fine sewing and enjoy working in miniature, you can apply your expertise to patchwork. This beautiful, doll-sized quilt is worked with 12mm (1/2in) hexagons.

Great care has been given to the choice of floral fabrics for the central design, achieving the effect of a wreath of flowers. The flower heads are all of similar size and to scale. The design is 'lightened' at the edges by the use of pale-coloured patches with small sprig motifs in browns and reds, to give the impression of ferns and tiny leaves. The leafy effect has been emphasised by working quilt ties on the outer points of the hexagons, on the right side of the work. A group of four flowered patches is set at each corner of the quilt.

Patches required

Finished size approximately 38cm (15in) square
Using a 12mm (1/2in) hexagon template: 343 cream patches; 125 patterned patches

Working the design

Work a double rosette of cream hexagons for the centre of the quilt, then join four 'rows' of patterned hexagons round the rosette, using a sprigged fabric for the outer patches. Continue working with cream hexagons to the edges of the quilt, setting a group of four flowered patches at each corner, as shown in the picture.

Finishing

Cut a piece of cream fabric 2.5cm (1in) larger all round than the finished patchwork. Press the patchwork with the papers in position, then remove the papers. Press the outer edges of the quilt again.

Turn and press a hem to the right side of the backing fabric, mitring the corners. Baste the patchwork to the fabric on the edges and then machine-stitch all round, following the shape of the hexagons and working 3mm (1/8in) from the edges.

Work quilt ties on the points of the outer row of flowered hexagons and on the points of the four flowered hexagons at each corner of the quilt.

Squares

Although squares are very adaptable shapes they are not the easiest to work with because they must be accurately cut and joined. From the square, rectangles and triangles are obtained geometrically and thus a varied range of patterns is possible.

Patterns with squares

Many of the traditional American block patchworks (see pages 62-63) are based on squares, triangles and rectangles and, by adding the diamond shape, endless patterns are created. Blocks are divided geometrically, as shown in Fig 1.

Joining squares

Squares can be joined by three methods. Machine-stitching, often used for making modern quilts, is quick and produces a strong finish. Hand-sewing, using small running stitches, is the traditional American technique. The third method is associated with English patchwork and uses paper templates (see overleaf). This method produces very accurate joins but is slow to work and is usually used only with small – 12-45mm (½-1¾in) – square patches.

Trip Round the World

This is a popular modern patchwork design and is made up of 5cm (2in) squares. In the quilt pictured, the arrangement of the patches leads the eye to see the squares as diamonds, and hand-quilting worked across the squares strengthens this impression. To vary the traditional design, rows of triangles have been worked around the central area of squares. The edges of the quilt are worked with Somerset patches (see page 28). The quilt measures 100cm (40in) square.

Patches required

Using a 5cm (2in) square template: 21 red, 4 grey, 12 yellow, 20 pale pink, 28 turquoise, 60 mid-blue, 52 deep pink, 34 pale blue patches

Using a 5cm (2in) triangular template: 64 royal blue patches 5×9cm (2×3½in) rectangles for Somerset patches: 8 of each of the above colours

Working the design

Join squares to make strips, then join strips in the sequence shown in the picture. Work triangles around the central area of squares and edge the quilt with Somerset patches.

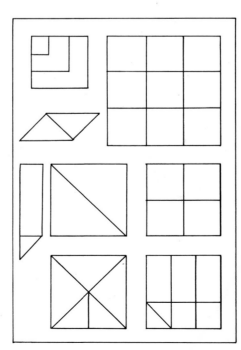

Fig 1 *Squares can be divided geometrically to make smaller squares, rectangles and triangles, and from these, other shapes can be formed*

Simply squared

Here are three easy things to make in patchwork using squares.

Pencil case

Patches required
Finished size of patchwork 20cm (8in) square

Using a 4cm *(1½in)* square template:
12 red patches; 13 patterned patches

Working the design
Join five squares into a strip. Alternate patches and rows to make a 20cm *(8in)* square.

Making the case
Cut a piece of lining fabric to the same size as the patchwork. Cut two circles in patterned fabric and two in lining fabric 7.5cm *(3in)* in diameter.

Baste one lining and one patterned circle together, one pair for each end of the bag.

Line the patchwork, then bind two sides with purchased bias binding.

Insert a zip fastener between the bound edges. Sew the circles into the ends of the bag, wrong sides together, trim the seam allowances and finish with bias binding.

Cushion

Patches required
Finished size 35cm (14in) square

Using a 5cm *(2in)* square template:
49 patches

Working the design
Sew seven squares together into a strip, then join seven strips to make a 35cm *(14in)* square.

Finishing
Cut a piece of fabric to the same size as the patchwork. Baste the two pieces together, right sides facing, inserting covered piping at the edges if desired. Machine-stitch on three sides and part of the fourth and turn to the right side. Insert a zip fastener if desired. Close the seam with slipstitches after inserting the cushion pad.

Dorothy bag

Patches required
Finished size 20cm (8in) deep, 12.5cm (5in) diameter

Using a 5cm *(2in)* square template:
28 blue patches; 21 white checked patches

Working the design
Starting with a blue square, join seven squares into a strip, alternating blue and white.

Make seven strips and join as shown in Fig 1 overleaf, staggering the rows.

Making the bag
Cut a piece of lining fabric to the same size as the patchwork. Cut two circles of fabric 14cm *(5½in)* in diameter. Cut two circles of card 11cm *(4½in)* in diameter.

Join the straight edges of the patchwork to make a cylinder. Join the edges of the lining in the same way. Slip the lining over the patchwork, right sides facing. Machine-stitch together round the top edges (on the dotted line shown in Fig 1 overleaf). Trim off the points

Mounting the square

The folds at the corners of squares are not difficult to make.
1. Fold the sides of the fabric patch on to the paper (Fig 1).
2. Fold down the top edge and hold the fold with an oversewing stitch. Take the thread to the opposite corner and hold the fold with an oversewing stitch (Fig 2).
3. Fold up the bottom edge and hold the fold with a stitch. Take the thread to the opposite corner and make a stitch to finish (Fig 3).
4. For large squares — from 5cm *(2in)* — it may be necessary to make another holding stitch in the middle of the fold, taking the needle through the fabric and the paper but not through to the right side of the patch (Fig 4).
5. To join patches, hold two squares together, right sides facing and matching corners exactly. Make a tiny oversewing stitch 3mm *(⅛in)* from the corner. (Pick up two or three threads of the fabric — you should be able to feel your needle just skimming the edge of the paper.)
6. Make a second stitch over the first, then move back to the corner and make a double oversewing stitch right on the corner.
7. Begin oversewing from right to left (left to right if you are left-handed), working over the stitches already made (Fig 5).
8. The third patch can be joined in without cutting the thread if desired. When stitching, take care not to catch the folds into stitches.

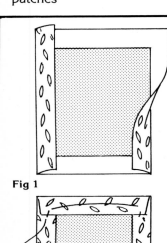
Fig 1

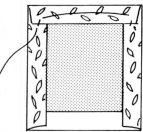
Fig 2

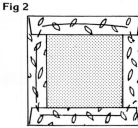
Fig 3

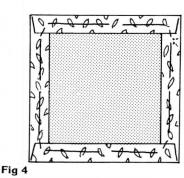
Fig 4

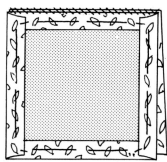
Fig 5

of the patchwork squares. Turn to the right side and press.

Gather the bottom edge and trim off the patchwork points. Baste the bottom of the bag to one of the fabric circles, right sides facing, adjusting gathering stitches evenly. Machine-stitch. Slip a piece of card under the seam allowances of the bottom of the bag and work long stitches across the card to hold it in place (Fig 2).

Cover the second piece of card with the second circle of fabric, gathering the fabric edges round the card. Pad with a little cotton wool. Slip this padded circle into the bottom of the bag when the bag is completed.

Drawstring top

Cut a strip of blue fabric (or use purchased tape or ribbon) and machine-stitch round the bag, about 4cm (1½in) from the top. Where the strip meets, thread through 1m (approx 1yd) of 3mm (⅛in) ribbon. Knot the ends and use as a drawstring to close the bag.

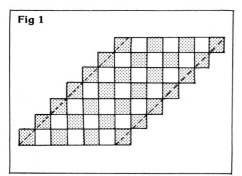

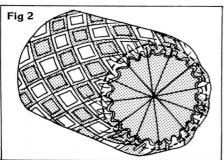

Fig 1 *Join strips of blue and white patches, staggering each row. The dotted line shows cutting line for top and bottom edges of bag*

Fig 2 *Slip a circle of card under the gathered seam allowances at the bottom end of the cylinder of fabric, then work stitches across to secure the card*

Star banner

This striking banner illustrates the varied designs and patterns that are possible when working with squares, triangles and rhomboids. All the shapes in this patchwork are shown on page 18, Fig 1.

The banner is designed with 12 blocks joined with strips, and with small squares at the intersections. The two halves of the quilt, from the vertical centre, are mirror images. The fabrics, chosen from the Laura Ashley range, are co-ordinated in colour and pattern, and this adds to the overall harmony of the design.

Fig 1 shows the panel broken down into its 12 blocks. The panel, finished with quilted strips of patterned fabric at the sides, measures approximately 75×60cm (30×24in).

Additional interest is given to the panel with hand-quilting. A double-leaf motif has been worked in the central block, on the four squares and two of the triangles surrounding the eight-point star. More double-leaf quilting motifs link the half-blocks above and below the central block. Straight lines of quilting have been used to bisect squares, and the play of light on these quilted patches adds to the textural effect of the finished patchwork.

Fig 1 *Diagram shows the banner's 12 blocks, made up of squares, triangles and rhomboids*

Fig 1

Strips and Rectangles

Fabric cut into rectangles or long strips can be used to produce many different effects. Log Cabin, a popular strip patchwork, is worked around a square and is an appliqué technique. Somerset patchwork, worked by folding rectangles, produces a three-dimensional effect. Strip patchwork is also a simple technique for making garments and fashion accessories.

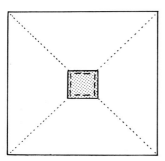

Fig 1 *Sew the chimney patch in the middle of the foundation square*

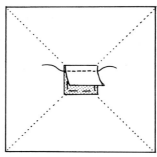

Fig 2 *Lay the first dark strip on the square, matching raw edges, and sew in position*

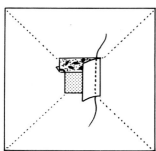

Fig 3 *Fold back the first strip and sew the second dark strip in position*

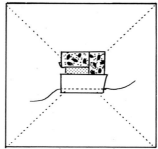

Fig 4 *Fold back the second strip and sew the third, light-coloured strip in position*

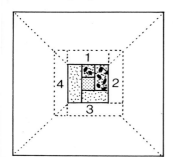

Fig 5 *The first round of four strips stitched and folded back. The dotted lines show the order in which the second round of four strips is worked*

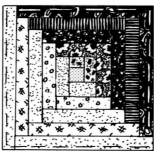

Fig 6 *Five rounds of strips complete the log cabin block. Baste all round the edges*

Log cabin

This is probably the best known of the old, American designs. As its name implies, the design is based on the traditional structure of a log cabin, the central square representing the chimney and the surrounding strips being the walls. One side of the block is worked in dark colours and the other side in light colours, depicting the firelight on the cabin walls and the shadows in the corners.

Log cabin can be made by hand or with machine-stitching and is worked on a foundation fabric in blocks. This means that fabrics of mixed weight can be used if desired.

Basic technique
Strips cut from light and dark fabrics are stitched in rows around the square.
1. Cut the foundation fabric 30cm *(12in)* square. With a ruler, pencil lines diagonally from the corners to mark the middle. Cut the chimney patch 5cm *(2in)* square and place this in the middle of the foundation square. The corners should lie on the pencilled lines. Work running stitches all round the patch (Fig 1).
2. Cut strips from light and dark fabrics, across the width, and 4cm *(1½in)* wide – 2.5cm *(1in)* strips plus seam allowances of 6mm *(¼in)*. Starting with a dark strip, lay it on the chimney square, raw edge to raw edge and right sides facing. Sew with small running stitches 6mm *(¼in)* from the edge, then cut away the strip level with the sides of the square (Fig 2).

3. Fold back the strip, away from the centre, and hold with pins. Turn the work. Using the same dark fabric, lay the second strip along the edge of the chimney square (see previous page, Fig 3). Position it from the corner of the square to the outer edge of the first strip. Sew, as before, with running stitches and cut off the strip. Remove the pins.

4. Fold back the second strip and hold with pins. Turn the work and, using the light-coloured fabric, lay the third strip along the square. Sew and trim as before, then fold the strip back (Fig 4).

5. Work the final strip of the first round in the same way and using the same light-coloured fabric (Fig 5).

6. Continue working round, keeping the light and dark strips to the same sides of the block as before, until you reach the edge of the foundation fabric (five rounds). Work basting stitches round the outside edge to hold the last four strips in place (Fig 6).

Log cabin quilt

The quilt in the picture has 32 blocks, joined to make eight rows of four blocks. The border strips are 20cm *(8in)* wide. The quilt has been mounted on a backing 4cm *(1½in)* larger all round than the finished patchwork, the edges taken on to the right side and hemmed.

The quilt has been finished with quilting lines (see page 17 for technique), worked diagonally across the blocks.

Shapes in harmony

The traditional Log Cabin pattern pictured on the opposite and previous pages inspired this wall panel but the techniques used in its construction are different. Nine blocks 20cm (8in) square make up the panel and each block is made by stitching strips of fabric into right angles around a corner square. The design has been planned so that attention is focussed on the apex of the panel, the darker tones being used in the lower blocks and the lighter towards the top corner.

To create movement in what might otherwise have been a rather static design, circles and arcs have been hand-quilted across the blocks. Instead of there being conflict between the two forms, a rhythmic harmony has been achieved.

Wall panel

Materials required
Finished size 91cm (36in) square
91cm (36in) square fabric for backing
4 strips 7.5×71cm (3×28in) for inner border
6cm (2½in) square fabric for each block
Strips for each block as follows:
Band 1: 1 strip 5×10cm (2×4in);
    1 strip 5×6cm (2×2½in)
Band 2: 1 strip 5×14cm (2×5½in);
    1 strip 5×10cm (2×4in)
Band 3: 1 strip 5×16cm (2×6½in);
    1 strip 5×14cm (2×5½in)
Band 4: 1 strip 5×20cm (2×8in);
    1 strip 5×16cm (2×6½in)

Working the design
Fig 1 shows the arrangement of strips for each of the blocks. Taking 6mm (¼in) seams throughout, machine-stitch two Band 1 strips to the edges of a square, then stitch Band 2 strips to the edges of the Band 1 strips. Continue with Bands 3 and 4 to complete the block. Make nine blocks, then machine-stitch together in the arrangement shown in the picture. Join the inner border strips to the edges of the patchwork, overlapping the strip ends.

Finishing
Lay the patchwork right side up on the backing fabric, centring it. Pin and then fold the edges of the backing on to the patchwork. Press the turnings under and hand-sew the edges of the backing to the edges of the patchwork, to make a border as shown in the picture.

The wall panel has been hand-quilted (see page 17 for technique) with circles over the corner squares and arcs across each block.

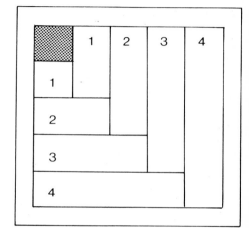

Fig 1 *Each block is made up of eight strips of fabric stitched together to make right angles around a corner square*

Strip patchwork cushion

The cushion in the picture is made in colours to tone with the wall panel. Strips are joined to make a 30cm (12in) square and two rows of Somerset patchwork (see page 28) add texture to the design. The finished size of the cushion, including the border, is 45cm (18in) square.

Somerset patchwork

Somerset patchwork is believed to have originated about a hundred years ago in the English county of that name. The effect is of chevrons, formed by folding rectangles of fabric. The folded patches are worked on to a foundation fabric in rows as pictured or in rounds, as shown on the green cushion on page 39.

Basic technique

1. Cut a rectangle of fabric on the straight grain 5×9cm *(2×3½in)*. Fold down a 6mm *(¼in)* turning on the top edge (Fig 1). Crease the fold with your thumb nail.
2. Bring the two top corners down to meet in the middle of the bottom edge (Fig 2). Press the patch lightly. To secure the patch, work two or three oversewing stitches 3mm *(⅛in)* from the bottom edge, through all thicknesses.

Coral cushion

A patterned and plain fabric in the same coral colour has been used for Somerset patches, worked in alternate rows.

Materials required

Finished size of patchwork before making up the cushion 34×32cm (13½×12½in)
38×35cm *(15×14in)* calico for foundation
63 rectangles 5×9cm *(2×3½in)* from patterned fabric; 54

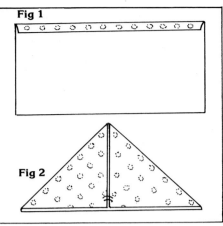

Fig 1 *Fold a 6mm (¼in) turning to the wrong side on the top edge of the rectangle*

Fig 2 *Bring the two top corners to the middle of the bottom edge. Oversew to secure*

rectangles of the same size from plain fabric
35×5cm *(14×2in)* strip of patterned fabric
Cushion backing fabric to size of finished patchwork
Covered piping if desired

Preparation

Fold, stitch and press rectangles to make Somerset patches.

Spread out the calico and pencil a line 5cm *(2in)* from the bottom edge. Baste the strip of patterned fabric to the calico, with the top edge along the pencilled line.

Working the design

Lay four patterned patches on the strip with the points 12mm *(½in)* from the bottom edge (Fig 3). Arrange a row of five patterned

patches between these, the points 2.5cm *(1in)* from the bottom edge of the foundation fabric (Fig 4). Pin these nine patches in position. Arrange a row of four plain patches next, positioned exactly over the patches of the first row, the points 2.5cm *(1in)* apart. Pin in place.

Sewing Somerset patches

Patches are secured to the foundation fabric by sewing from the point of one patch to the point of the patch below, inserting and bringing up the needle between the folds so that the thread does not show. Work two or three backstitches to secure each point. Secure the outer edges of each patch by working backstitches across each corner (Fig 5).

Work 13 rows, alternating fabrics and securing patches as described.

Finishing

Trim the finished patchwork, cutting off the points of the patches that extend beyond the edges of the foundation fabric.

Make up the cushion by stitching the front piece to the back piece, leaving part of the seam open for inserting a cushion pad. Stitch piping into the seam if desired. Close the open seam with slipstitches.

Working with a sewing-machine

Somerset patches can be applied to the foundation fabric with machine-stitching, working row by row. Machine-stitch right across the straight edge of each row of patches, then catch the points down by hand.

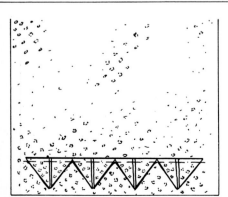

Fig 3 *Arrange four patches in a row, 12mm (½in) from the bottom edge*

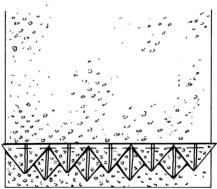

Fig 4 *Add five patches, positioning them between the patches in the first row, and pin*

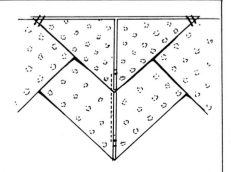

Fig 5 *Sew patches to foundation fabric by inserting and bringing up needle between the folds and working from the point of one patch to the point of the patch below. Catch down the outer corner with backstitches*

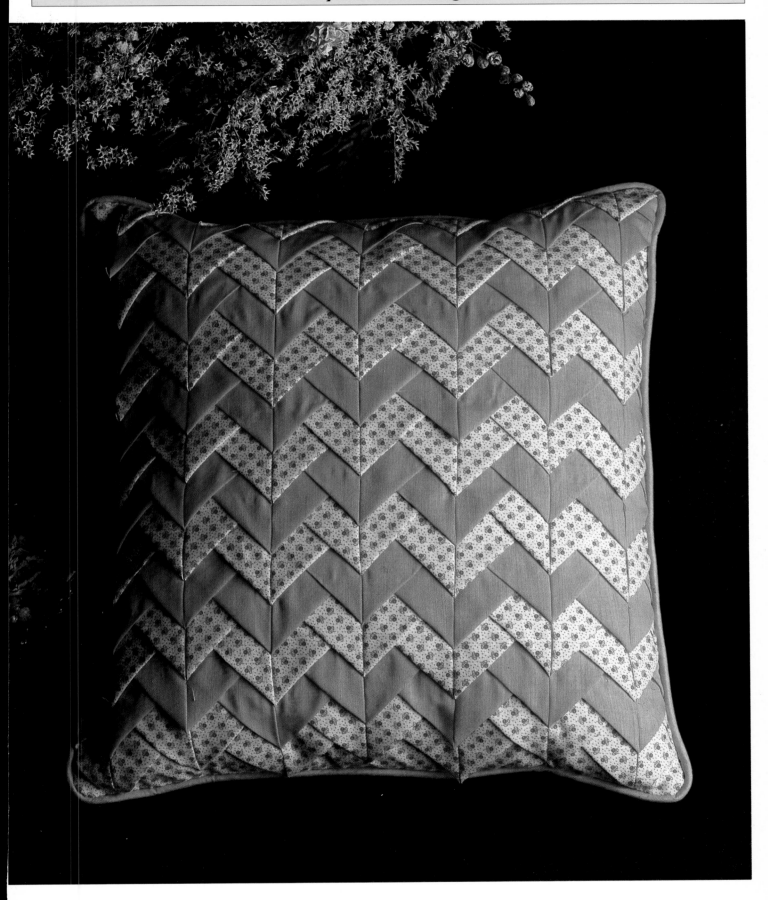

Patchwork for fashion

Patchwork can be used to make beautiful clothes and fashion accessories – simply choose a paper pattern and work areas of patchwork to the approximate shapes of the pattern pieces. Almost all of the patchwork designs in this book could be worked for garments – hexagons for boleros or jackets, with a matching hexagon trim on a skirt edge; diamonds in satin for a beautiful evening coat; squares of cotton for bright skirts or for children's clothes; crazy patchwork perhaps for a man's robe, or in suede or leather for a glamorous bag and matching hat.

There are a few points to watch when working patchwork for clothes and accessories.

Fabrics

If the garment is to be laundered the fabrics used for patchwork must be washable and colourfast. If dry cleaning is likely, then fabrics can be mixed more freely but care must be taken to ensure that weights of fabric are similar and that all patches are cut on the straight grain to prevent distortion in the finished work.

Patchwork for clothing must be lined. The lining makes a strengthening base fabric and prevents patches pulling away from each other in wear.

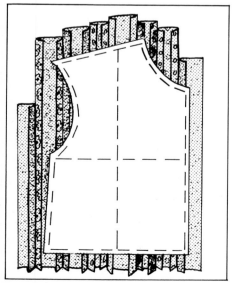

Fig 1 *Baste the lining to the patchwork vertically and horizontally, then all round edges*

Preparing patchwork for dressmaking

Use the paper pattern to cut out the garment in lightweight lining fabric. Now work the patchwork to the approximate shape of the lining pieces. Catch the lining to the patchwork vertically and horizontally with basting stitches, then baste all round the edges (Fig 1). Trim the patchwork to shape. Make up the garment with the two fabrics as one. For a neat and finished look inside the garment, you will need a second, loose lining, worked in the usual way.

Surface decoration

If the finished patchwork is to be embroidered, or appliquéd with lace or ribbons as shown on the jacket pictured, this should be done after the garment has been made up so that any decoration can be worked over seams.

Finishing edges

In most cases, patchwork garments will be finished according to the garment pattern, with the lining caught to the turned hems of the patchwork. In very simple garments, such as the jacket pictured, the edges can be neatened with bias binding or a soft braid. Apply the binding to the right side on the edges, trim the edge back to 6mm (¼in) seam allowance, then finish the binding on the wrong side.

Strip patchwork jacket

This simple, edge-to-edge jacket, with cap sleeves, scooped neckline and no bust darts, is an ideal pattern for patchwork. The shoulder detail, worked in bands of ribbon and lace, gives the effect of a raglan sleeve, which adds interest to the jacket shape.

The jacket is made up with fabric strips in different colours and widths – the easiest type of patchwork for a garment – and is worked with machine-stitching.

Hand-quilting has then been worked between the strips, and cut-out motifs of lace appliquéd at random to the garment. The jacket is lined and the edges finished with a silky braid.

Working with suede and leather

Suede and leather, and materials simulating these, are often used for patchwork clothes and accessories. They are fairly easy to handle and can be worked either by hand or by sewing-machine, depending on the item being made.

If square or rectangular shapes are being used, and they are of reasonable size – from 5cm *(2in)* – patches can be cut with seam allowances and machine-stitched together right sides facing, in the usual way. The seam allowances are pasted down on the wrong side of the patchwork when it is completed.

Generally, however, whatever the shape, suede and leather patches are cut out without seam allowances. Use the metal template, scissors or a sharp crafts knife and a metal rule.

Patches can be joined with zigzag machine-stitching, using a wide zigzag stitch set fairly closely to a satin stitch effect. Alternatively, use zigzag stitching supplemented with straight stitching worked across seams after the patches have been joined to strengthen the seams (Fig 1). Hold patches, edges touching, for stitching.

Hand-sewing is possible on both suede and leather, using oversewing stitches worked along the edges of two patches held together right sides facing. However, this technique is not recommended for clothing where there is likely to be some pull on the patchwork.

Crazy patchwork

Crazy patchwork techniques (see page 54) work well with suede and leather, patches being overlapped on the edges and topstitched with zigzag or straight machine-stitching. Mixing suede and leather with other fabrics is not recommended.

Fig 1

Diamonds

There are two kinds of diamond, the lozenge diamond and the long diamond.
The long diamond is the more difficult of the two to work because it has two fine
angles of 45° and two of 135° and fabric must be carefully folded when
mounting patches. The lozenge diamond has two 60° and two 120° angles.

Tumbling Blocks bag

Three lozenge diamonds, each worked in a different tone and joined together, give the optical illusion of a cube shape. The design based on this is called Tumbling Blocks. The bag in the picture is made of grey, white and black fabric, maximising the cube effect.

Basic technique

Three lozenge diamonds are sewn together to make a cube effect (Fig 1). Fig 2 shows the arrangement of the diamonds for making the bag. The design is the same on both sides of the bag.

Materials required

Finished size 38×35×10cm (15×14×4in)
Using a 10cm *(4in)* lozenge diamond template: 14 white patches; 16 grey patches; 16 black patches
50cm *(20in)* of 120cm *(48in)*-wide calico lining
38cm *(15in)* of 120cm *(48in)*-wide black fabric

Working the design

Sew patches together to make the area shown in Fig 2. Make two pieces of patchwork, for front and back of bag. Press open seam allowances on the edges.

Preparation for the bag

Trim each piece of patchwork as shown in Fig 2 to 40×38cm *(16×15in)*. Baste the patchwork on the edges to calico lining cut to the same size.

Cut a strip of the black fabric 12.5cm *(5in)* wide by 38cm *(15in)* long for the base of the bag. Cut two strips of black fabric each 12.5cm *(5in)* wide by 40cm *(16in)* long for the bag's sides. Baste all three pieces on to pieces of calico cut to the same size. Work black fabric and calico as one.

Cut two strips of black fabric each 4cm *(1½in)* wide by 38cm *(15in)* long for binding the bottom edges of the bag.

Cut four strips each 4cm *(1½in)* wide by 40cm *(16in)* long for binding the side edges. Cut a strip 4cm *(1½in)* wide by 99cm *(39in)* long for binding top edges of the bag. Cut four strips of black fabric each 5cm *(2in)* wide by 33cm *(13in)* long for the bag's carrying straps.

Making up the bag

Baste the bag base to the bottom edges of the bag, wrong sides facing (Fig 3). Use the prepared strips to bind these edges, machine-stitching through all thicknesses from the right side of work.

Baste the side pieces to the bag front and back and to the base piece. Bind the edges with the prepared strips, machine-stitching.

Making the straps

Press the long edges of each prepared strip to the middle so that they meet. Press in the short ends 6mm *(¼in)*.

Baste two strips together, seam allowances to the inside, then topstitch close to the edges all round.

Bind the top edge of the bag with the prepared strip, joining ends at a corner. Stitch the straps to the top edge, as shown in the picture.

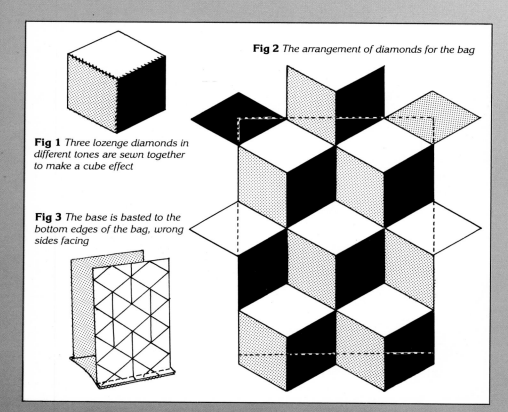

Fig 1 *Three lozenge diamonds in different tones are sewn together to make a cube effect*

Fig 3 *The base is basted to the bottom edges of the bag, wrong sides facing*

Fig 2 *The arrangement of diamonds for the bag*

Long diamond

The long diamond is often used in conjunction with the square and the triangle. It is more difficult to work than the lozenge diamond but, successfully used, can make a stunning centrepiece for a patchwork.

The difficulty in working lies in the very sharp points of the long diamond. In mounting the fabric to the paper shape it is necessary to make three folds on each point to accommodate the fabric. This can make the point very bulky, which, in turn, may make it difficult to achieve a perfect join with other diamonds.

When working long diamond patterns, care should be taken in the choice of fabric as the sharp point of the paper shape can pierce the fabric. Closely woven cottons or silks are recommended.

Star of Bethlehem

The Star of Bethlehem, made entirely of long diamonds, is a well-known and popular pattern on both sides of the Atlantic and can be used for large pieces of work, such as quilts and wall hangings, or as a centrepiece for smaller designs.

The tablecloth in the picture has a basic star shape set into the main background fabric. The cushion has a star in the centre surrounded by squares and half-squares (triangles) to make a square piece of patchwork suitable for a cushion cover.

Any size long diamond template can be used to work the Star of Bethlehem pattern. The tablecloth uses a template with 5cm (2in) sides and the cushion uses a 4cm (1½in) template.

The Star of Bethlehem pattern is an eight-point star formed by joining together eight diamond-shaped segments (Fig 1). Each of the eight segments is made up of 16 long diamond patches (Fig 2).

Traditionally, five different colours or patterns, or tones of a colour, are used in the arrangement illustrated in Fig 2: The tablecloth and cushion in the picture are worked using the Star of Bethlehem technique but the arrangement of tones is different from the traditional pattern.

Patches required

For traditional Star of Bethlehem
40 light tone
16 1st middle tone
24 2nd middle tone
16 dark tone
32 darkest tone

Working the design

Following Fig 2 for the arrangement of patches, start at the widest point of the segment and join two darkest tone patches to a 2nd middle tone patch. Join two more darkest tone patches to a 2nd middle tone patch. Join in two light tone patches as shown and then join the two resulting diamond shapes of four patches with a 2nd middle tone and a light tone patch. Work from this area towards the points of the segment, following the arrangement shown in Fig 2.

When all eight segments have been worked, join two segments, then two more together. Join the two groups to make half of the star. Join the two halves to make the complete Star of Bethlehem.

Mounting the long diamond

When practising folding and mounting, use a fine, crisp fabric, such as cotton, and crease the folds sharply with your thumb nail.

1. Fold and crease fabric on side A-B to the left (Fig 1).
2. Fold and crease fabric on side B-C to the left, making a corner fold at B (Fig 2). Secure the fold with two backstitches.
3. Fold and crease fabric on side A-D to the right. Trim off the 'tail' of excess fabric at A (Fig 3). Secure the cut edge of fabric with a backstitch as shown.
4. Fold down the point of fabric at A (Fig 4), then fold again to the left to make a neat point (Fig 5). Secure with a backstitch.
5. Fold and crease the fabric on side D-C to the right, making a corner at D and securing it with backstitches (Fig 6).
6. Trim the 'tail' of excess fabric at C as before (stage 3, Fig 3). Then double-fold the point at C (as before), securing with backstitches (Fig 7).

Fig 1   Fig 2   Fig 3   Fig 4   Fig 5   Fig 6   Fig 7

Fig 1 *The Star of Bethlehem is an eight-point star made up of diamond-shaped segments*

Left: Tablecloth and cushion worked in Laura Ashley fabrics, using the Star of Bethlehem pattern

1st middle tone

light tone

2nd middle tone

darkest tone

light tone

dark tone

1st middle tone

Fig 2 *Each of the diamond-shaped segments is made with 16 patches, in light, middle and dark tones*

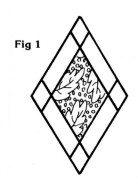

Fig 1

Jane Austen's quilt

This very fine patchwork quilt is worked using two sizes of lozenge diamond, and a rhomboid shape for the light-coloured 'trellis' effect dividing the diamonds. The quilt was made by Jane Austen with the help of a sister and their mother at the beginning of the nineteenth century. It can be seen displayed in Jane Austen's house in the village of Chawton, Hampshire, in southern England.

The Austens used a 5×2.5cm (2×1in) rhomboid between the diamonds, with the result that there are joins where one feels there should not be joins. This has been overcome in the instructions given here for making a similar quilt, by using a 9×3cm (3½×1¼in) rhomboid and a 3cm (1¼in) diamond. Thus, each large diamond will have a rhomboid sewn to each of the four sides and a diamond to each point (Fig 1).

Patches required

For reproducing a Jane Austen quilt, finished size 236×155cm (93×61in)
Large central diamond 33cm (13in) along each side.
Using a 9cm (3½in) lozenge diamond template: 232 flowered patches; 22 flowered patches cut in half lengthwise; 24 flowered patches cut in half across the width
Using a 3cm (1¼in) lozenge diamond template: 2200 patches in bright, mixed fabrics; 323 patches in light-coloured spotted fabric
Using a 9×3cm (3½×1¼in) rhomboid template: 282 patches in light-coloured spotted fabric

Working the design

Fig 2 shows one quarter of the quilt. It is recommended that patchwork begins with the large, central diamond, which is cut from a floral fabric. Around this are set the rhomboids and the small diamonds in the light-coloured, spotted fabric. Work the patchwork outwards from this central diamond. If the quilt is being made as a group project, the border area could be worked as four strips and joined into the main quilt on completion.

Finishing

The Jane Austen quilt is lined with cotton fabric, the edges of the patchwork border turned under 2.5cm (1in). It is recommended that the quilt be tied to prevent ballooning (see page 16 for technique).

Fig 2

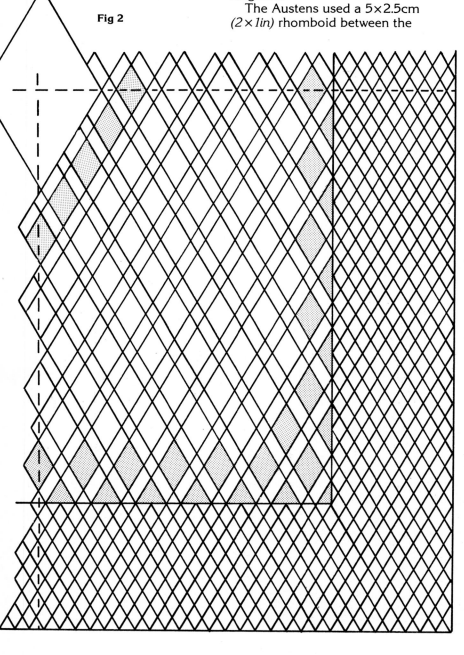

Fig 1 *Bad joins can be avoided by sewing a rhomboid to each side of the diamond and a small diamond to each point*

Fig 2 *One quarter of the Jane Austen quilt, showing the arrangement of diamonds and rhomboids*

Mixing Shapes

Once you have mastered the art of patchwork using the five basic shapes — the hexagon, square, rectangle, diamond and triangle — you can start mixing shapes and creating your own designs.

Designs in mixed shapes

If you have a few mounted patches left over from projects you can experiment with them to make mixed-shape designs. Spread them out on a cork board and move them around into different combinations. When you have achieved the desired effect you can spear the patches into the cork with pins. You will find that many shapes can be fitted together, depending on the angles of the corners or points and the lengths of the sides.

Fig 1 is an example of how one small shape can be built up into a circular pattern. In the middle is a 12mm (½in) hexagon. Round this are irregular pentagons, with their short sides 12mm (½in). Into the angles are fitted 2.5cm (1in) hexagons with irregular pentagons in between, arranged on their long sides.

Diamonds could have been used to surround the central design in Fig 1 instead of hexagons and irregular pentagons, and the design continued with diamonds and triangles (Fig 2).

Fig 3 shows the completed motif, the edges finished with half elongated hexagons. This design could be used for a quilt or a wall panel, or it would make an unusual hexagon-shaped cushion.

Right: The red and white cushion is worked with diamonds, church windows, squares and octagons. The blue cushion is worked with hexagons and rhomboids. The green and white cushion is made with Somerset patchwork (see page 28) worked in the round

Fig 1 *A round design made with hexagons and irregular pentagons*

Fig 2 *The same central arrangement as Fig 1, surrounded with diamonds and triangles instead of hexagons and irregular pentagons*

Fig 3 *The completed motif, with more triangles and diamonds added and finished at the edges with half elongated hexagons*

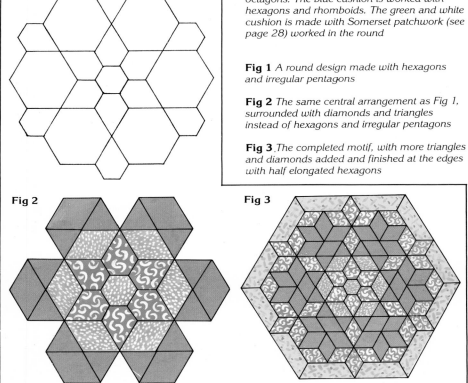

Fig 1

Fig 2

Fig 3

Octagons and squares

The octagon cannot be worked without other shapes and is most often used with the square. By adding long diamonds (Fig 4) or church windows (Fig 5), more interesting patterns are possible.

One of the most interesting patterns worked with octagons is Interwoven Ribbons (Fig 6). Rectangles and triangles are joined to make pointed strips and these are set around octagons and squares.

The blue cushion pictured on the previous page has another form of this pattern, worked with hexagons and rhomboids. The rhomboids each have a row of machine embroidery worked down the middle, and this inspired touch helps to emphasise the effect of ribbons.

Church windows and coffins

These two shapes are distorted forms of the hexagon. Church window has six equal sides, four shallow angles and two right angles. Coffin has two sides that are a different length from the other four and all the angles are the same.

Although church window can be used alone it is rarely seen worked in this way. More often, it is combined with the hexagon and the square. However, worked alone, the shapes can be arranged to give the effect of a 'rosette' (Fig 7), which might be used as the foundation for an adaptation of the popular Grandmother's Flower Garden quilt design (see page 12).

The red and white cushion

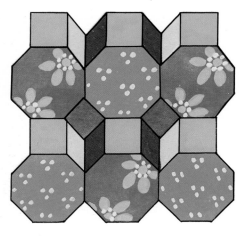

Fig 4 *Octagons, squares and long diamonds*

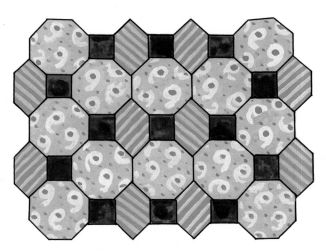

Fig 5 *Octagons, squares and church windows*

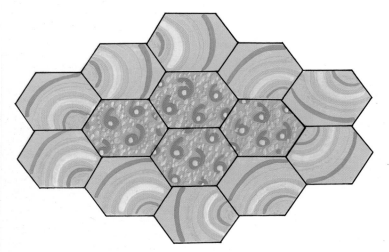

Fig 7 *Church windows set into a 'rosette'*

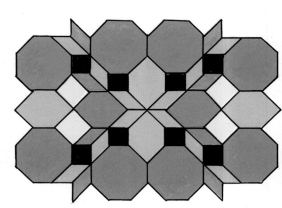

Fig 8 *Church windows, diamonds, squares and octagons*

pictured on the previous page uses diamonds in the middle with church windows fitted into the angles. Patterned diamonds and squares form the next round, followed by a plain round of octagons and church windows. The design of octagons and squares is continued right to the edges of the cushion.

This type of design takes time and patience to work out. If you are planning a similar, complicated arrangement of shapes, it is very useful to have draughtsman's isometric paper on which to draw your design.

Fig 8 is a design made up of church windows, diamonds, squares and octagons. Worked in a range of toning colours and patterns, it would be suitable for making a large area of patchwork for covering stools or small chairs, or for a bedhead.

The coffin is not a popular shape and is rarely used, although it is easy to work with. Fig 9 illustrates a three-dimensional effect achieved with coffins and rhomboids.

Motifs with shapes

Motifs for cushions or for quilt blocks can be built up around a geometric shape to look rather like flowers. Here are two combinations to try.

Aunt Martha's Rose Set six squares to the sides of a hexagon. Set diamonds between the squares. Set triangles on each of the squares.

Wedding Tile Make up six squares, each containing three rectangles in different colours. Set the squares around a plain-coloured hexagon. Set triangles between the squares.

Fig 6 *Octagons worked with rectangles, triangles and squares to make the Interwoven Ribbons design*

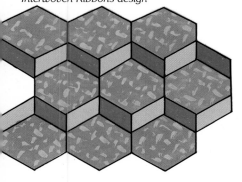

Fig 9 *Coffins and rhomboids produce a three-dimensional effect*

Pentagon ball

The five-sided pentagon requires the use of other shapes, such as the diamond, to make a piece of flat patchwork. Pentagons used alone and joined together make a ball structure.

Materials required

Finished size 20cm (8in) diameter
Using a 6cm *(2½in)* pentagon
   template: 12 patches
Polyester filling

Working the design

Stitch five pentagons around a sixth to make half of the ball (Fig 1). Work six more pentagons in the same way. Fit the two half-balls together, right sides facing, and oversew the seams, leaving two open for inserting the filling (Fig 2). Turn to right side and finish patchwork as instructed on page 10.

Insert the polyester filling and close the open seam with oversewing or slipstitches.

More ideas with pentagons

The technique described above can be used to make felt balls for children (Fig 3), round pincushions, filled with cotton wool (Fig 4), round sachets, filled with dried herbs or lavender (Fig 5), or, if worked in suede or leather, to make balls for games (Fig 6).

If fabric patches are mounted on thin card and the card is left in place after patches have been sewn together, a rigid ball structure is obtained. This can make an attractive hanging Christmas decoration (Fig 7). Work several in seasonal colours, with sparkling beads, sequins, braids, etc sewn or glued to the sides of the ball.

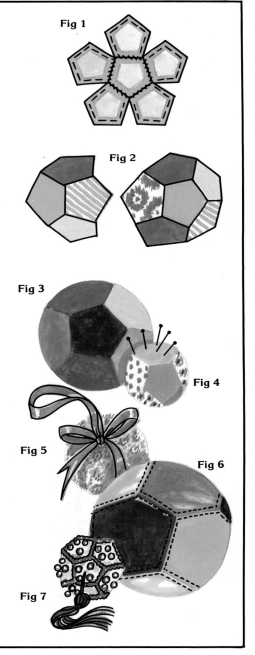

Fig 1

Fig 2

Fig 3

Fig 4

Fig 5

Fig 6

Fig 7

Red carry bag

The bag is made up of seven blocks of patchwork stitched together on the diagonal, with triangles set to complete the rectangular shape (Fig 1). The patchwork is machine-stitched but could equally well be worked with hand-sewing if preferred.

Fig 2 shows the construction of each block. The four component shapes are given to scale in Fig 3, so that the templates can be drawn.

The bag pictured is piped with bias-cut fabric but the instructions given here omit the piping.

Materials required

Finished size of patchwork 91×50cm (36×20in)

75cm *(30in)* of 120cm *(48in)*-wide cotton lining fabric
2 63cm *(25in)* zip fasteners
For each block: 4 triangles (A); 8 triangles (B); 4 half elongated hexagons (C); 4 church windows (D)
For filling sides and corners: 10 triangles (A)

Working the design

Make up seven blocks and join with machine-stitching as shown in Fig 1. Join triangles at corners and sides as shown. Trim the patchwork to 94×53cm *(37×21in)*.

Making up the bag

Cut a piece of the lining fabric to the same size as the patchwork. Baste together on the edges, wrong sides facing.

Make the gusset from the same fabric. Cut and join two strips 7.5×145cm *(3×57in)*. Baste them together, wrong sides facing, on one long side. Machine-stitch a seam at

Fig 1 *Seven patchwork blocks stitched together on the diagonal, with triangles set at the corners and sides. The rectangular shape is the cutting line for making up the bag*

both ends of the strip, 4cm *(1½in)* long. Insert the zip fasteners so that they meet in the middle. (If it is necessary to use two shorter zip fasteners, adjust the length of the end seams accordingly.) Unpick the basting stitches. Make up the bag as shown in Fig 4, stitching in the gusset and taking 12mm *(½in)* seams.

(If piping is being used, insert this in the seams now.)

Handles

From the same cotton lining fabric cut four strips 7.5×30cm *(3×12in)*. Press 6mm *(¼in)* turnings on all four sides of the strips. Pin two strips together, wrong sides facing, and machine-stitch all round 3mm *(⅛in)* from the edges.

Topstitch the straps to the top of the bag, on each side of the zip fasteners.

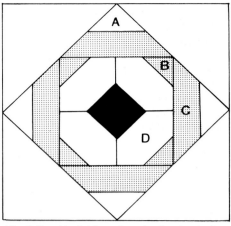

Fig 2 *One block of patchwork, showing how the four component shapes – A, B, C and D – are joined together*

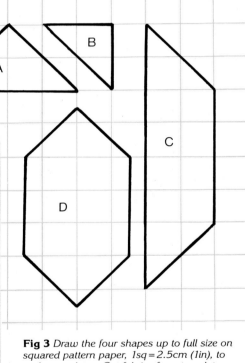

Fig 3 *Draw the four shapes up to full size on squared pattern paper, 1sq = 2.5cm (1in), to make templates. Cut fabrics from templates, adding 6mm (¼in) seam allowance all round*

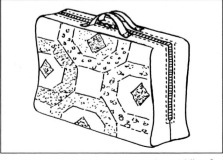

Fig 4 *The zip fasteners meet at the middle of the bag top. The handles are stitched each side of the zip fasteners*

Fig 1 *Geometric shapes can be combined to make many designs*

Geometric pictures

Creating pictures from patchwork is a fascinating way of working with geometric shapes. All the shapes — rectangles, squares, hexagons, triangles, rhomboids and diamonds — can be combined in different ways to make designs (Fig 1).

Children's books, with their simplified images, are a useful source of ideas. Trace the motifs, copy them on to squared paper, enlarging the design, then draw geometric shapes over the design to select the templates you will use to translate the motif into patchwork.

If pictures for framing are being worked fabrics should generally follow the design concept — for instance, velvet for grass, lacy patterns for trees and bushes, silk and satin for shiny surfaces. If the picture is for applying to a fashion garment, make sure the fabrics used are washable.

Red cats panel

The Red Cats panel pictured is worked entirely in geometrically-shaped patches — squares, rectangles, half elongated hexagons, triangles and rhomboids (see detail, Fig 2). Only four fabrics have been

used — a plain red, a plain green, a white sprigged and a green sprigged.

Each cat motif is 30cm *(12in)* tall and the entire panel measures 114×75cm *(45×30in)*.

Cat motif

The cat motif has been abstracted in Fig 3 and the component patches identified. These can be drawn up on squared paper and then transferred to card or the smooth side of fine-grade sandpaper to make templates for working the cat. (Sandpaper is ideal for templates, as it does not slip when used rough side down on the fabric.)

The cat motif, used singly, could be worked into patchwork or applied to a plain fabric background. It is of a size to make a cushion cover or a block for a quilt. Worked in pastel colours in small-motif patterned fabrics, the cat blocks would make a charming quilt for a child.

Fig 2 *Detail of Red Cats panel*

Fig 3 *Each cat is made with the following shapes:*
A *Seven 2.5cm (1in) triangles (note: the triangles for the cat's tail are arranged in two different ways — see detail, Fig 2)*
B *Six rectangles 2.5×5cm (1×2in)*
C *Two half elongated hexagons 2.5×7.5cm (1×3in)*
D *Two half elongated hexagons 2.5×12.5cm (1×5in)*
E *One 7.5cm (3in) square*
F *Two rectangles 7.5×2.5cm (3×1in)*

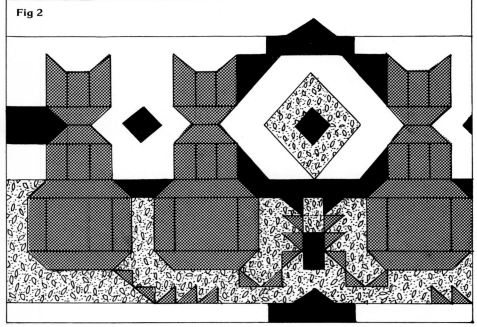

Fig 2

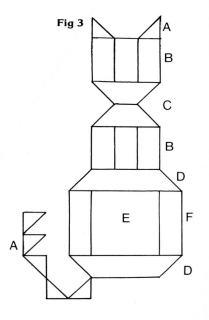

Fig 3

Non-geometric Shapes

The patchworks in this chapter are called 'non-geometric' because they are not based on any of the traditional shapes. Clamshell and cathedral window are techniques that require careful cutting and sewing, while Suffolk Puffs can be considered a patchwork 'quick-make'.

Clamshell

Clamshell patchwork is a complex technique but, like many things well done, it looks simple when it is finished. Clamshell cannot be mixed with other shapes but the patches can be arranged in interesting patterns. The tea-cosy on this page and the needlework tidy overleaf both use the same basic clamshell technique (see also overleaf) to make a pattern known as Fish Scale.

Tea-cosy

Patches required
Finished size 25×30cm (10×12in)
Using a 5cm *(2in)*-wide clamshell template: 25 red patches; 15 deep pink patches; 12 flesh pink patches; 12 pale pink patches

Working the design
Following the technique for Assembling Clamshells overleaf, arrange three pale pink patches in a row. Work 11 rows as shown in Fig 1.

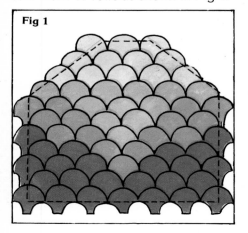

Fig 1 Arrangement of the clamshell patches for the tea-cosy front

Fig 2 Diagram for the tea-cosy pattern: A-A measures 30cm (12in); A-B measures 17.5cm (7in); B-C measures 14cm (5½in); C-C measures 7cm (2¾in)

Making up the tea-cosy
Draw a pattern up to full size on squared pattern paper from the diagram (Fig 2). Cut out the paper pattern, adding 12mm *(½in)* seam allowance all round. Pin the paper pattern to the finished patchwork and cut out the shape.

Using the same paper pattern, cut out one back from plain fabric, two lining pieces and two from thin wadding.

Baste the wadding pieces to the wrong side of the patchwork front and the back piece. Machine-stitch front to back with right sides facing and leaving bottom edge open. Trim back the wadding almost to the stitching line. Turn to right side and press.

Make up the lining, right sides together. Trim seam allowance to 6mm *(¼in)* and slip into the tea-cosy. Hand-sew the bottom edges together, turning in the seam allowance.

Fabric-covered piping can be inserted between the front and back pieces and into the bottom edge if desired.

Mounting the clamshell

The clamshell differs from other shapes that use papers in that the fabric is attached to the paper on the upper, curved edge only. The patches are arranged in rows to overlap the concave shape of the patch.

Although paper can be used for the backing shape, medium-weight, non-woven, iron-on interfacing works very well and is recommended. The term 'paper' is used in these instructions.

The seam allowance of the fabric shape is gathered round the top of the paper. For this reason, a thin fabric is best — a fine dress cotton or silk.

1. Using a plastic or metal template, draw round the outline on interfacing. Cut out 17 shapes.

2. Using a window template, so that you can see the area of patterned fabric you want, cut out 17 fabric clamshells. Make sure that the straight grain of the fabric lies down the centre of the clamshell and the crossways grain lies across the shape from side to side. Press the interfacing papers to the wrong side of the fabric shapes, following manufacturers' instructions, and leave to cool so that they are well fixed (Fig 1).

3. Run tiny gathering stitches round the concave shape of the clamshell, working fairly close to the edge. Draw up the gathering so that the fabric lies flat over the interfacing on the wrong side and fasten off the thread end. Even out the gathers round the shape and press flat. Make sure that you have a smoothly rounded shape with no peaks or points (Fig 2).

Assembling clamshells

Place six mounted clamshells in a row on a piece of plain fabric, right side up and with the edges just touching. Place a ruler across the top to make sure they are level, then pin in position.

Place five more clamshells into the semicircles formed by the first row, overlapping them by 6mm (¼in) and covering all the raw edges. Check to make sure they are straight. Work basting stitches around each clamshell in the second row about 1.5mm (¹⁄₁₆in) from the edge, attaching them to the first row (Fig 3).

Add a third row of six clamshells, in the same way. Rows of clamshells can be added to these foundation rows as desired, basting them in position.

Sewing clamshell patchwork

A small hemming stitch is used to sew one row to another, working on the right side of the work. These stitches must be worked as small as possible or the finished effect will be spoiled.

Finishing

When the area of patchwork required is finished, remove the basting stitches but leave the interfacing in place. Interfacing is particularly suitable when using thin fabrics, as it prevents both the seam allowance from showing through the finished work and the gathered surplus on the underside of the clamshell from marking the top surface.

Needlework tidy

The needlework tidy is designed with two pockets and hangs over the arm of a chair. The roll across the middle is for pins and needles. Like the tea-cosy pictured on the previous page, the tidy is worked in rows of clamshells in the Fish Scale pattern.

The tidy pictured is lined with a piece of mixed-shape patchwork but the instructions here use a plain cotton fabric for both the lining and the backing.

Materials required

Finished size 45×20cm (18×8in)

2 pieces of 50×25cm (20×10in) cotton fabric for lining and backing

2 pieces of 25cm (10in) square cotton fabric for lining pockets

50×25cm (20×10in) non-woven interfacing

2 pieces of 25cm (10in) square non-woven interfacing

12 strips 2.5×10cm (1×4in) of mixed fabrics

1 packet of 12mm (½in)-wide purchased bias binding (or cut 2.5cm (1in) strips on the bias from cotton fabric)

60 patches using a 5cm (2in)-wide clamshell template

Preparation

Draw the pattern (Fig 1) up to full size on squared pattern paper. Mark in the pocket division lines.

Use the paper pattern to cut out the lining, backing and interfacing. Trim one pocket shape from the pattern and put aside for later use.

Working the design

Following the techniques for mounting and assembling clamshells, set and sew 30 patches in seven rows, as illustrated in Fig 2. Make up two pieces of clamshell patchwork, both exactly the same.

Pincushion roll

Machine-stitch the 12 strips of fabric together on the long edges. Fold around a roll of cotton wool and slipstitch the edges together. Machine-stitch across the ends to close and flatten them (see picture).

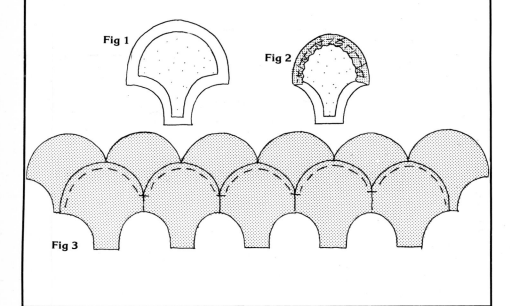

Fig 1

Fig 2

Fig 3

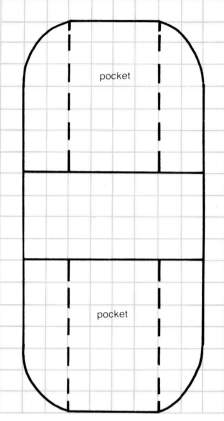

Fig 1 *Graph pattern for the needlework tidy, 1sq = 2.5cm (1in). The dotted lines indicate the stitching lines for the pocket dividers. A 6mm (¼in) seam allowance all round is included in the pattern*

Fig 2 *The pockets are made up of 30 clamshells sewn in seven rows. The dotted line indicates the pocket shape, cut with the pocket pattern from Fig 1*

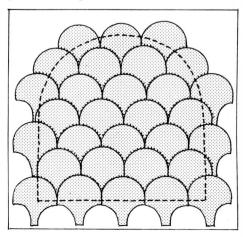

Making up the tidy

Baste the two pieces of patchwork to the pocket linings, wrong sides together and with the interfacing sandwiched between. Following the paper pattern for the pocket, pencil the lines for the pocket dividers on the lining side and machine-stitch.

Using the paper pattern, cut both pockets to shape. Bind the top, straight edge of both pockets with bias binding.

Baste the lining to the backing, wrong sides together and with interfacing sandwiched between. Pin and baste the pockets in place, matching the curves. Sew the prepared pincushion roll across the middle of the tidy, trimming ends if necessary.

Machine-stitch all round the tidy, stitching 6mm (¼in) from the edge. Bind all the edges of the tidy with bias binding.

Cathedral window

Cathedral window is a most effective form of patchwork, giving, as its name implies, the appearance of a stained glass window. The finished effect looks as though it is a difficult technique but, in fact, it is quite simple to work.

Cathedral window requires no lining and because each patch is applied to a foundation square and stitches are worked through all thicknesses, the whole piece is thereby quilted. The front of the work has the appearance of coloured windows and the reverse has a pretty, quilted effect. Cathedral window patchwork is therefore ideal for wall hangings or small quilts but probably looks best hung against the light, used as a window panel or blind as pictured.

Fabrics

It is usual to choose a plain colour, such as white or cream, for the foundation as this contrasts well with the inset coloured or patterned patches and displays the subtle folds of the 'frames' to good effect. You may prefer to choose a patterned fabric for the foundation and a plain for the patches, but whichever scheme you decide on, use it throughout the piece. Mixed effects do not work well.

The foundation patches for cathedral window are 15cm (6in) squares of fabric folded down to 7cm (2¾in) squares. Quite a large quantity of fabric is therefore required for this type of patchwork.

Estimate fabric carefully and buy all you need at one time as plain colours can vary in tone and the variations will show in the finished piece.

A considerable amount of the work in cathedral window patchwork lies in folding and re-folding the fabric, so you need to choose a fabric

that takes creases easily. However, make sure it is a fabric that requires no ironing. Cathedral window patchwork should not be ironed after laundering as this crushes the folds.

The patterned inset patches are only 4.5cm (1¾in) square and, provided the fabrics are washable and colourfast, almost any small scrap can be used.

Basic technique

1. Cut 15cm (6in) strips across the width of the plain fabric, on the exact grain of the fabric. Then cut the strips into 15cm (6in) squares, again making sure that you cut on the straight grain. The squares must be cut true to grain to ensure easy folding.
2. Cut 4.5cm (1¾in) squares from patterned fabric.
3. Press a 6mm (¼in) turning on all four sides of the plain squares (Fig 1). Fold each square and crease the fold lines with your thumb nail to mark the centre.
4. Fold the corners of the square to

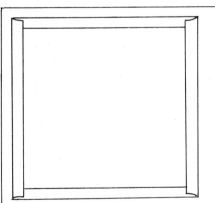

Fig 1 *Turn a 6mm (¼in) hem on all four sides of the square and press*

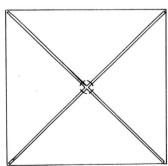

Fig 2 *Fold the corners of the square to the centre and press. Backstitch all the corners*

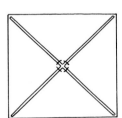

Fig 3 *Fold the corners of the new square to the centre and backstitch*

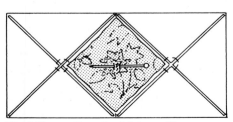

Fig 4 *Pin a patterned patch in position*

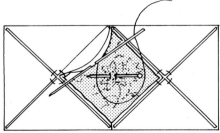

Fig 5 *Roll the folded edge over the patch*

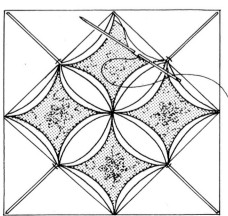

Fig 6 *Work slipstitches along folded edge*

the centre and press the folds. Backstitch the four corners together in the centre and the four outer corners, to hold them in place (Fig 2).

5. Take the corners of this new square to the centre and press again. Backstitch the points together in the centre, first vertically, then horizontally, and taking the needle through all thicknesses of fabric. You have now completed one foundation square which should measure 7cm (2¾in) (Fig 3). Make several more foundation squares.

6. Using small oversewing stitches, join four squares, wrong sides facing, to make a block. Take particular care to match the corners.

7. Pin the first patterned patch over the seam between two joined squares (Fig 4).

8. Starting in the middle of the folded edge of the foundation square, where there is the maximum amount of 'give' in the fabric, roll — or draw — the edge over the patch for about 3mm (⅛in) and taper it off to a neat point at the ends (Fig 5).

9. Work a double backstitch at each point, across the two converging sides. Then work very fine slipstitches along the rolled edge through all thicknesses of fabric (Fig 6).

10. Continue joining squares and applying patches to them in the same way. Do not sew too many foundation squares together before applying the patches or you will have too much fabric in your hand to work comfortably.

Cathedral window panel

The panel in the picture has 96 foundation squares, set 12 down and 8 across. A total of 2.85m (3¼yd) of 120cm (48in)-wide fabric is required for the squares.

There are 58 yellow patches, 28 green patches, 56 flowered patches and 30 sprigged patches.

On the outside edges of the panel, where there is insufficient space for a complete square, the folded edges of the foundation squares are drawn or rolled on to themselves and slipstitched in place.

Suffolk puffs

Suffolk Puffs are traditionally made up for bed covers and backed with a brightly coloured fabric that shows through the spaces between the puffs. They can also be used to make charming fashion garments, such as sleeveless jackets, skirts or shawls, and delightful toys, such as the clown shown below.

Basic technique

1. A circle of fabric is required to make each puff. Use a saucer or small plate as a template for the shape, measuring about 15cm (6in) in diameter. Cut circles and turn a 3mm (⅛in) hem to the wrong side. Press.
2. Using a strong fine thread, work tiny running stitches round the folded hem (Fig 1).
3. Pull up the thread tightly and finish off the end with a backstitch. Press the puff flat (Fig 2).
4. Join puffs together using four straight stitches worked side by side (Fig 3). It is traditional to use matching thread but a contrasting thread is permissable.
5. Suffolk Puff quilts should be tied at intervals, when lining is completed, to prevent ballooning. Work quilt ties (see page 16 for technique) through the middle of puffs.

Puff the Clown

An attractive doll can be made with Suffolk Puffs of different sizes worked in brightly coloured cotton fabrics.

Use 15cm (6in) circles for the puffs for the lower body, 12.5cm (5in) circles for the upper body, arms and legs, and 10cm (4in) circles for the wrists and ankles. Thread the finished puffs on fine string or doubled strong button thread, or use three or four strands of round elastic to make a jumping clown (Fig 4).

Make the head from two 12.5cm (5in) circles of fabric sewn together and stuffed with polyester filling. Make the hair from knitting wool and the hands and feet from felt.

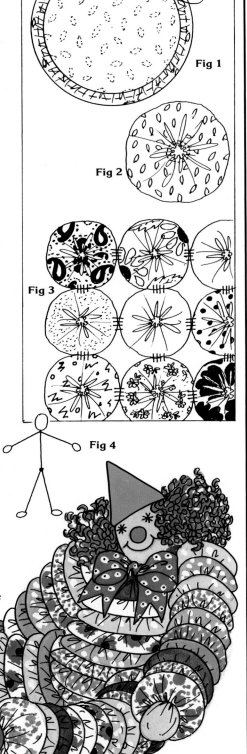

Puffed patchwork

Puffed and padded patchwork takes several forms. The eiderdown in the picture is made by working a piece of squared patchwork, then mounting it on a backing fabric and inserting a polyester filling in between. Another form involves making individual square or round 'bags' of fabric, stuffing them with filling, closing the 'bags' and then sewing them together on the edges to make warm, lightweight coverlets.

Both of these techniques are evolved from a much older method, Suffolk Puffs patchwork. A design originally from Suffolk in East Anglia, it is also known in the north of England and dates from the mid-eighteenth century. In America it is a traditional pattern and is called Yo Yo.

Baby's puffed eiderdown

The eiderdown in the picture was made for a baby basket or cradle and, filled with polyester filling, it is both lightweight and warm.

Preparation

To make a similar eiderdown, you need 56 15cm (6in) squares of washable fabric sewn together so that

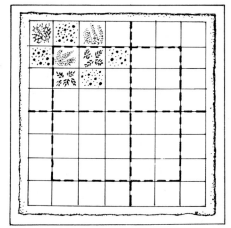

Fig 1 Work basting stitches across the middle of the patchwork, then down between the third and fourth row of patches. Work basting all round edges

the patchwork has eight rows of seven squares.

Cut a piece of backing fabric to the same size as the patchwork and cut a sheet of wadding or polyester filling 5cm (2in) larger all round.

Working the design

Place the backing fabric right side down. Cover it with the wadding or polyester filling so that 5cm (2in) overlaps the edges all round. Lay the patchwork on top, right side up, matching edges with the backing.

Work a line of basting stitches across the middle of the patchwork, from side to side and along the seam line between two rows of patches,

working through to the backing. Work a line of basting from top to bottom between the third and fourth row of patches. Now work basting stitches between the two rows of patches on the edges all round, through to the backing (Fig 1). Trim off any excess wadding or polyester filling at the edges.

Machine-stitch or hand-quilt between the squares of patchwork, working on the seam lines of the squares. Remove basting stitches.

Finishing

From the backing fabric, cut and join strips 20cm (8in) wide for a frill. For a reasonably full frill you will need approximately 6m (6⅝yd).

Fold and press along the length. Gather one edge and apply it to the right side of the quilt edges, right sides together. Fold the frill edge over to the wrong side of the quilt. Gather the other long edge, turn the edge under and hand-sew to the backing.

Patchwork and Appliqué

Patchwork and appliqué go hand in hand in quilt-making, the straight lines of seamed patchwork contrasting with the freedom of cut-out fabric shapes sewn to a foundation fabric. Crazy patchwork, the oldest of the techniques used to make new fabric from old, is still a thrifty craft and can be worked with different kinds of fabric to make items that are both beautiful and useful.

Crazy patchwork

The technique of sewing together small scraps of good fabric to make a larger piece has been practised for hundreds of years. Early examples of crazy patchwork were made of pieces of woollen fabric sewn together over a foundation fabric to make warm bed covers. Crazy patchwork as a decorative form of needlework, used to make dramatic quilts like the one pictured, evolved in the mid-nineteenth century.

The quilt pictured was made in the United States of America in the 1880s and is unusual in that it has been constructed from 12 blocks of patchwork, each individually worked and measuring 30cm (12in) square.

Fabrics

Although almost any kind of fabric can be used for crazy patchwork it is advisable to choose pieces of uniform thickness. If crazy patchwork is intended for making fashion garments or accessories that are likely to be subjected to heavy wear, it may be better to buy new fabrics, as partially-worn cloth may pull away from the stitches.

Foundation fabrics should be new; closely woven cotton is recommended.

The backing fabric, on which the crazy patchwork is mounted, can be of almost any type – velvet, woven wool, needlecord, brocade, heavy satin, twilled fabric or cotton – provided that it is of sufficient weight to support the patchwork.

Threads

All-purpose polyester thread is recommended for sewing the patches on to the foundation fabric. Stranded cotton or lustrous embroidery cotton are both suitable for the surface decoration. Tapisserie wools can also be used for textural contrast.

Preparation

Clean and press all patchwork fabrics. Iron creases from the foundation fabric.

Working the design

Although crazy patchwork may look haphazard in design, consideration must be given to the position of patches to achieve a pleasing balance of colour, texture and pattern.

Cut pieces of the patchwork fabrics to the size required and lay them on the foundation fabric, moving them around until a harmonious effect is achieved. Starting at a corner, trim the first selected piece to a right angle. Pin it to the corner, then work running stitches around the right angle, taking stitches through the foundation fabric (Fig 1).

Slip the next patch about 12mm (½in) under the edge of the first. Work running stitches around the edges of both patches, leaving the front edges free so that you can slip more patches underneath (Fig 2). Continue adding patches, slipping them under the edges of previous patches and sewing securely to the foundation fabric through all layers. Work across the foundation fabric until it is covered.

Embroidery

Any kind of stitch can be used in crazy patchwork. Stitches are worked over the raw edges of all the patches to secure them and to make a decorative effect. The quilt pictured uses Chain Stitch, Feather Stitch, Herringbone Stitch, Buttonhole Stitch and Cretan Stitch.

Finishing

Mount the finished patchwork on a backing fabric (see page 16 for technique).

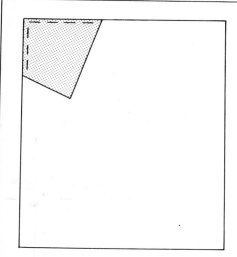

Fig 1 *Trim the first patch to a right angle and sew to a corner*

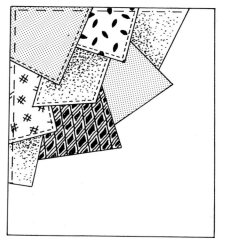

Fig 2 *Slip patches under the edges of the first, then sew through all layers, leaving the front edges free for inserting more patches*

Friendship quilt

Making Friendship Quilts is an American tradition and one of the most charming of communal sewing projects.

In the days of the early American pioneers, young girls, who were engaged to be married, set to stitching quilts and covers for their future homes. Twelve quilts were considered sufficient to set up housekeeping but a thirteenth quilt was made by the betrothed girl's friends, each working a block of appliqué or patchwork. The blocks were designed in a variety of ways, illustrating events from the girl's life, or depicting flowers, insects and animals from the locality.

At the final quilting bee, an important social occasion in the community and to which the men were sometimes invited, the blocks were 'set', joined with strips of fabric or prepared patchwork, and then the quilt was mounted in a frame for hand-quilting.

The modern quilt in the picture was made for an American girl living in England by friends in a local quilting group. It was designed by the owner in three main colours: green, white and pink. A free hand was given to those making the blocks, working within this colour scheme. Some of the blocks are made in traditional patterns, others have been adapted and are loosely based on popular designs (Fig 1).

The quilt measures 218×142cm (86×56in) and each of the rectangular blocks is 22×29cm (8½×11½in). The blocks are set in strips of green and white fabric. The outer strips surrounding the blocks are made up of 5cm (2in) green squares at the corners, white rectangles measuring 29×5cm (11½×2in) and green rectangles measuring 10×5cm (4×2in). The inner strips are wider: the green squares are 10cm (4in) and the green and white rectangles are 29×10cm (11½×4in). The completed patchwork quilt is bordered with a 10cm (4in) band in green fabric.

Quilting has been worked on the blocks and linking strips to add texture. The traditional Twisted Ropes design is used for some of the quilting (Fig 2).

Fig 1

1	2	3
4	5	6
7	8	9
10	11	12
13	14	15
16	17	18

Fig 1 *Key to the designs of the blocks that make up the Friendship Quilt pictured:*
1 *Elongated Star* **2** *Twin Sisters* **3** *Dutchman's Puzzle* **4** *Rail Fence* **5** *Dresden Plate*
6 *Adaptation of Windmill* **7** *Birds and Flowers*
8 *Woven Ribbons* **9** *Double Hearts*
10 *Checkerboard* **11** *Adaptation of Fan* **12** *Star*
13 *House* **14** *Squared pattern* **15** *Tulips*
16 *Log Cabin* **17** *Flower* **18** *Log Cabin*

Fig 2 *Twisted Ropes quilting design*

Fig 2

Patchwork motifs

Pieces of patchwork can be used as appliqué motifs to decorate clothes and accessories, and home furnishings. Hexagons, sewn into rosettes, or the Ocean Wave pattern on page 12 make pretty borders. Diamonds, triangles and squares are all suitable for grouping into motifs.

Preparation

After sewing patches together, press on the wrong side with the papers still in position. If the right side of work needs pressing, unpick the basting stitches but leave the papers in place. Dry-press over a thin cloth. If the patchwork fabrics are thin and the turnings show through on the right side, it will be necessary to line the entire piece or to cut 'papers' from cotton lining fabric or thin, non-woven interfacing and insert them under the turnings before working appliqué.

Lining motifs

Pin the pressed patchwork to a piece of cotton lining fabric and pencil round the shape. Cut out the lining 6mm (¼in) away from the pencilled line. Press open the turnings on the edges of the patchwork. Baste the patchwork to the lining, right side down. Machine-stitch on the pencilled line, leaving a small gap for turning to the right side. Close the open seam with slipstitches and press the lined motif ready for appliqué.

Mounting appliqué

Appliqué can be worked either by hand or by machine. To hand-sew, work tiny slipstitches through the edge of the patchwork motif (Fig 1). Machine-stitching can either be done with a small straight stitch, worked right on the edge of the patchwork, or with an open zigzag stitch.

Fig 1

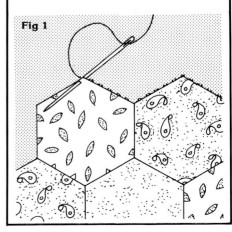

Country cottage

The picture combines two techniques, traditional English patchwork using hexagons and appliqué for the cottage and path. The hexagons are worked as a mosaic of plain and patterned fabrics chosen to represent trees, flowers and foliage, sky and clouds. In places, diamonds and smaller hexagons have been superimposed on hexagons to add detail or more interest to the pattern.

Working the design

The panel measures 91×60cm (36×24in) and is made up of approximately 225 hexagons worked with a 2.5cm (1in) template.

The trees and foliage are worked in dark blue sprigged fabric and in different tones of brown plain and sprigged fabrics. The flower beds are made with hexagons in red, white and pale blue flowered fabrics. Flower motifs have been cut out and backed with iron-on interfacing to stiffen them, then sewn to the flower beds, with the petals left free of the background.

The hills behind the cottage are worked in cream and beige patterned hexagons, and the sky in blue-grey, with pale blue and pink and white hexagons for clouds.

Appliqué and embroidery

The cottage shape is worked separately (Fig 1). The roof, windows, door and chimney are applied to the cottage shape, then embroidery is worked to define details. Tiny broderie flowers fill the window box.

The garden path is also appliquéd and is outlined with embroidery stitches in black thread.

Surface embroidery has been worked on some of the hexagons. The sky patches, for instance, have been given texture with running stitches. Tree trunks and branches are outlined in embroidery and the cottage smoke has beads added for sparkle. A picket fence is embroidered in red.

Quilting

Panels of this type of patchwork need to be quilted so that when they are hung there is a play of light on the different areas of the design. Both machine-stitched and hand-sewn quilting have been worked (see page 17 for technique), adding interest and texture to the picture.

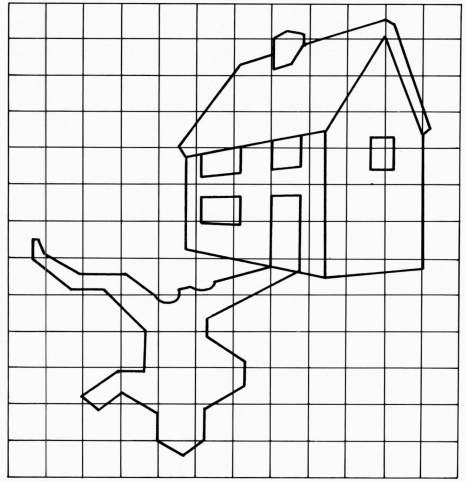

Fig 1 *Draw the cottage and path on squared pattern paper to scale 1sq = 5cm (2in). Draw the outlines on thin card or fine sandpaper and cut the shapes in fabrics with a regular motif (see picture). Use the scaled-up drawing to cut patterns for the cottage roof, window, door and chimney*

Appliqué ideas

The cottage in the picture is stitched to the background fabric using an appliqué technique. The entire motif could also be used as an appliqué design for a plain fabric cushion, with perhaps surface embroidery added for flower beds. The cottage would also make an ideal appliqué design for a block quilt, and each cottage could be worked in different colours.

Quick appliqué

For cushions and quilts, an iron-on interfacing material – Bondaweb – can be used for a quick appliqué technique. It is available by the metre, 44cm (18in) wide. Cut the motif shape from the bonding material and, following manufacturers' instructions, press the appliqué motif over the cut-out interfacing shape to the base fabric.

Iron-on patchwork

The same appliqué technique can be used for a quick patchwork effect.

Spread the Bondaweb on the base fabric and arrange the cut-out patchwork pieces on the bonding material, edges touching exactly. Press, following the manufacturers' instructions, making sure that the patches adhere firmly. If the item being worked is to be laundered the edges should be stitched down with zigzag machine-stitching worked over the joins or with straight stitches worked 3mm (1/8in) from the edges.

Grandmother's Fan

Grandmother's Fan is a pattern that adapts well to modern colour schemes. Traditionally, a mixture of printed and plain fabrics were used for the fan, usually in pretty pastels, and blocks were 30cm (12in) square. The panel pictured has been made with 23cm (9in) blocks, set five across and four down.

Red fan panel

Materials required

Finished size 140×165cm (56×65in)

60 11cm (4½in)-long fan segments in red fabric

60 11cm (4½in)-long fan segments in red and white print fabric

2.30m (2½yd) of 120cm (48in)-wide dark blue fabric

1.40m (1½yd) of 120cm (48in)-wide yellow fabric

2.30m (2½yd) of 120cm (48in)-wide red fabric for backing

20 25cm (10in) squares of muslin for foundation squares

Preparation

Cut 20 25cm (10in) squares from the dark blue fabric. Cut 20 small fan shapes, 9cm (3½in) long on the straight edges, from one corner of each square. The remainder of the square will be used for the corner of each block. Cut bias strips 2.5cm (1in) wide from the yellow fabric to edge each fan shape (see picture).

Working the design

Baste the first fan segment right side up to the muslin foundation square

7.5cm (3in) from a corner, aligning raw edges (Fig 1). Join subsequent segments on the long edges, right sides together, using machine-stitching or running stitches. Alternate plain red and printed fabrics (Fig 2).

As each segment is joined, press the segment flat to the foundation fabric. Do not press seams open.

Baste down the last segment's edge.

Turn a 6mm (¼in) hem on the curved edge of the small blue fan shape, clipping into the seam allowance for a smooth curve (Fig 3a). Baste, then hem over the top edge of the large fan (Fig 3b).

Lay the blue corner piece on the foundation square, matching raw edges, then pin and baste. Trim the

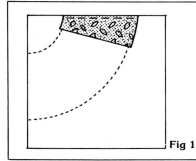

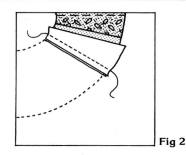

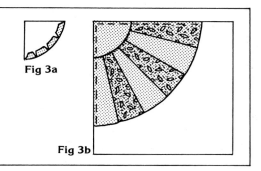

Fig 1 *Baste the first fan segment to the foundation square, matching raw edges and setting the segment 7.5cm (3in) from a corner*

Fig 2 *Alternating fabrics, sew segments together, right sides facing, with running stitches or machine-stitching*

Fig 3a *Clip into the seam allowance on the curved edge of the small blue fan piece*
Fig 3b *Baste, then hem the curved edge of the fan over the top edge of the large fan shape*

inside edge to follow and touch the curved edge of the fan. Sew with running stitches. Turn the edges of the yellow bias strips under and hem over the join between the dark blue background and the red fan.

Finishing

Join blocks together with machine-stitching or running stitches, setting blocks five across and four down, as shown in the picture.

Cut 9cm *(3½in)*-wide strips from yellow fabric for the inner border, butting ends at the corners. Cut 16cm *(6½in)*-wide strips from blue fabric for the outer border, butting ends at the corners.

Cut 25cm *(10in)* strips across the width of the red fabric and join to a long side to make a piece 145×170cm *(58×67in)* for backing.

Interline the quilt (see page 16) and mount on red fabric, turning and hemming the edges on the front of the panel.

Pieced patchwork

Piecing was the term used originally in eighteenth-century America for the practice of sewing scraps of partly-worn fabric together to make new fabric for quilts and wall coverings.

Fabric pieces were cut into geometric shapes based on the square, the triangle and the diamond and, from these, imaginative patterns were stitched.

Hundreds of different pieced patchwork designs are on record and early American history can be traced through them, some signifying political events, others being reminders of customs, people and places. Some are illustrated overleaf.

Although many of the traditional patterns are based on geometric shapes, appliqué is also part of American piecing traditions. Dresden Plate, Basket and Grandmother's Fan are examples of piecing and appliqué used together.

Planning designs

The designs illustrated are all square blocks. They can be drawn to scale to any size desired. The most popular-sized block for quilts is 30cm *(12in)* square but blocks can be 25cm *(10in)* or even 20cm *(8in)* square.

To reproduce these designs you will need squared or isometric paper, coloured pens or pencils, a ruler and a protractor.

Decide first the finished size of the block and then the scale to which you will be working on your squared paper. You might, for instance, decide that one square of your paper is going to represent 2.5cm *(1in)* and that you will work a 25cm *(10in)* block. The outline for your block will therefore be drawn over 10 small squares by 10 small squares. Missouri Puzzle is a 25-patch block so for this design you need to divide your block into 25 smaller squares. Copy the design into your square and then colour in areas to represent the fabric colours you will be using. If a block has a complicated design, made up of very small patches, you may need to use a scale of one square representing 12mm *(½in)*.

If you are planning a design that

has combined techniques (appliqué and piecing), such as Basket, you will need to copy the non-geometric shapes freehand.

The next stage is draw to full size all the various shapes that make up the block, to make templates.

Fig 1 shows the 25-patch Missouri Puzzle with the various component shapes abstracted. Still working on squared paper, measure and draw all the shapes in your chosen block, taking particular care to see that the sides of shapes which touch others are of exactly the same measurement and that angles are true, otherwise the block will not be square when patches are sewn together.

Making templates

Templates are used for cutting fabric patches and in piecing, a template is used again and again and must remain accurate in size throughout.

A stiff, quality card is the most popular material used. Some patchworkers like to use linoleum for

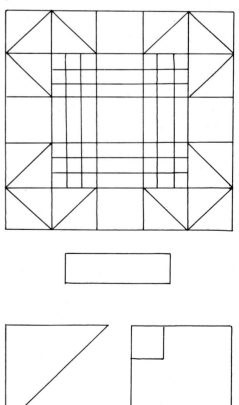

Fig 1 *Draw the block to scale on squared paper. To make templates, draw each shape in the block to full size*

templates, and fine-grade sandpaper is also recommended. The rough surface of the sandpaper adheres to the fabric and does not slip when shapes are being drawn.

Trace the full-size drawing of each shape on to the template material. Alternatively, you can paste the squared paper drawing on to the template material and cut out both together. Use a sharp crafts knife and a ruler to cut out templates.

Estimating fabric quantities

It is important to estimate the amount of fabric required for a pieced quilt before starting the project. To do this, you must first work out how many patches of each shape are to be cut from each fabric colour. Working from your coloured-in block and having decided on the number of blocks you intend to have in your finished quilt, you can estimate the quantity of patches of each kind required.

The Missouri Puzzle block, for instance, has 36 small squares, 12 rectangles, 5 large squares and 24 triangles. If you were planning a quilt with this design and with 20 blocks, you would multiply each of these quantities by 20.

Following the method for estimating fabric quantities on page 14, work out the number of patches that can be cut from the width of fabric and the number of rows of patches that can be cut from the length. Remember that you will need extra fabric for borders, etc.

Using templates

Working with a sharpened, medium-hard pencil (or tailors' chalk for dark fabrics), lay the template on the wrong side of the fabric at top left (but not touching the selvedge). Hold the template down firmly and draw round it. Move it to the right and draw the next shape 18mm (¾in) away. Always keep at least 18mm (¾in) between shapes for ease of cutting out. Draw all the patchwork pieces of one shape and from the same fabric at the same time. Cut patches out with scissors, working 6mm (¼in) away from the pencilled line. Count them carefully and then string them on a length of thread for safe-keeping.

Grandmother's Fan

Robbing Peter to Pay Paul

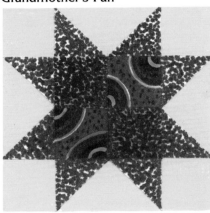
Saw-toothed Star

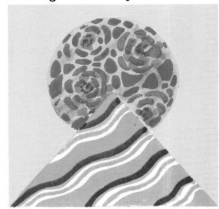
Moon Over the Mountain

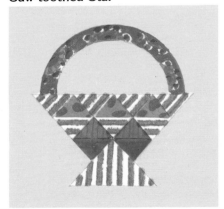
Basket

Lightning

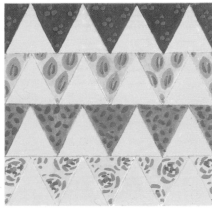
Dog's Tooth

Pinwheel

Dresden Plate

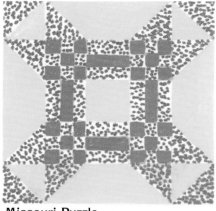
Missouri Puzzle

Sewing

When sewing patches together, join them in the simplest way and do not attempt to fit a piece into an angle. Join small patches together first to make a larger patch, then join to larger patches to make strips (Fig 1). Finally join strips together to make the complete block.

If you are using the traditional method of sewing by hand, begin and end with a backstitch and work small running stitches along the marked seam line. Work a few oversewing stitches at corners first to ensure exact joins (Fig 2).

After the block is completed, press it on the wrong side with a medium-hot iron, pressing the seams flat.

Blocks are joined together in strips, then the strips are joined. This can be done with running stitches, taking 6mm (¼in) seams, or, if you prefer, with machine-stitching.

Kansas Trouble

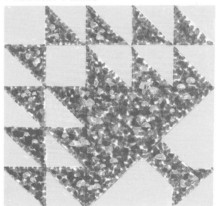
Pine Tree

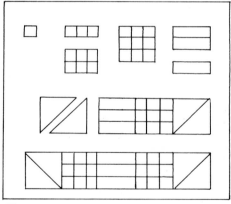

Fig 1 *Join small patches first, then join them to larger patches to make strips*

Fig 2 *Join corners of patches with oversewing stitches to ensure accurate joins, then work small running stitches along the pencilled seam line, beginning and ending with a backstitch*

Lemon Star

Crown of Thorns

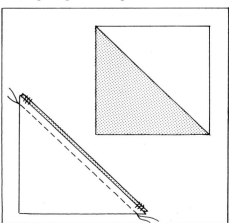

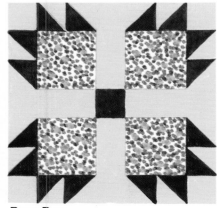
Bear Paw

Mountain Pink

Making templates

Although templates for patchwork are widely available, you may occasionally need to make your own. Use a firm cardboard that will withstand wear, or have the templates cut in hardboard.

When you are using hand-made templates, remember that these are for cutting papers. When using them to cut fabric, add 6mm (¼in) seam allowance.

Materials and equipment required

You will need a pair of compasses, a protractor, steel ruler, cutting board, sharp crafts knife, HB pencil and some firm cardboard.

Hexagon

The sides of a hexagon are equal to the radius of its circle. Thus, for a 2.5cm (1in) hexagon, set the compasses to 2.5cm (1in) and draw a circle. Without changing the measurement, place the point of the compasses at any point on the circle and mark off to each side on the circle. Move the compasses to one of these points and mark again.

Continue until you have made six equidistant marks. Join the points A-B, B-C, C-D, D-E, E-F, F-A (Fig 1).

Square

Rule a line to form the base of the square. Place the protractor on this line and mark a right angle (at 90°). This line is the perpendicular. Measure the required length on both lines and mark these points A and B (Fig 2). Place the protractor at point A and mark a right angle (90°). Measure this line to the same required length and mark the point C. Join C-B to complete the square.

Rectangle

Work as for the square but make the two horizontal sides longer than the vertical sides. The long sides are usually twice or three times the length of the short sides.

Lozenge diamond

Draw a hexagon as shown in Fig 1. Mark the centre point O. Join E-O, C-O and A-O to make three diamonds (Fig 3).

Octagon

Draw a base line and then a perpendicular, as for the square (Fig 2). Where the lines meet mark point

A (Fig 4). Using the protractor, mark an angle of 22½° and join to A. Measure the required length and mark this point B. At B, using the protractor, mark an angle of 45° and join to B. Measure the same required length and mark this point C. Continue marking angles of 45° and measuring the required lengths until an eight-sided shape is drawn.

Long diamond

Draw an octagon as shown in Fig 4. Mark the centre point O. Find the radius of the circle with the compasses. With the point of the compasses at point E mark an arc outside the hexagon (Fig 5). Place the point of the compasses at D and mark another arc, crossing the first arc. Mark the point X. Join X-E, X-D, E-O, D-O.

Pentagon

Draw a base line X-Y and a perpendicular H-A (Fig 6). With A as the middle, and using the protractor, mark an angle of 36° and draw the line to the required length. Mark the point B. At B mark an angle of 72°. Draw a line to length and mark the point C. Continue in the same way, to points D, E and A, to make the five sides.

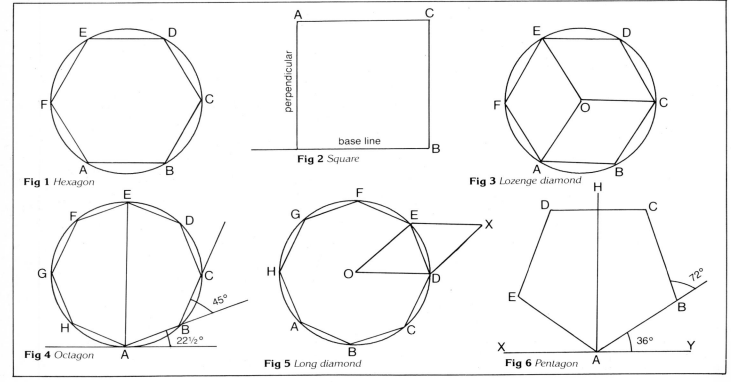

Fig 1 *Hexagon*

Fig 2 *Square*

Fig 3 *Lozenge diamond*

Fig 4 *Octagon*

Fig 5 *Long diamond*

Fig 6 *Pentagon*